Videodrome

Scene-by-Scene

Videodrome
Scene-by-Scene

John David Ebert

© 2016 John David Ebert
All rights reserved

ISBN: 9781530202928

Acknowledgements

Special thanks go to J.D. Casten and Lawrence Pearce.

Cover artwork:
"Oblivious" by Lawrence Pearce (2016)

Contents

On Luminous Screens
& Other Electron / Neuron Assemblages   13

Opening Title Sequence   25

Samurai Dreams   29

Harlan   33

The Rena King Show   37

Pittsburgh   43

Nicki Brand   47

Masha   51

Cigarette Burn   55

Max and Masha   59

Cathode Ray Mission	63
The Videocassette	69
Archives	75
Gun / Orifice	81
Barry Convex	85
Corpse / Corpuscle	93
Programming Max	97
Gun Embryo	101
Spree Killer	105
The Video Word Made Flesh	109
Killing Harlan	115
Spring Trade Show	119

The New Flesh	125
Notes	131
Bibliography	143

"When the phantom becomes real, reality becomes a phantom."

--Gunther Anders

On Luminous Screens
& Other Electron / Neuron Assemblages

Luminous surfaces: today, everywhere one looks, we are surrounded by self-luminous electronic video screens. They come in all shapes and sizes from the tiny rectangular squares of our smartphones to the gigantic advertisements on the sides of buildings in downtown Shanghai. And now they are *all* digital: television has become LCD or plasma-based, while celluloid has disappeared inside the matrix of a virtual data file.

But back in 1983, when David Cronenberg's first great masterpiece *Videodrome* was released in January of that year—it had originally been scheduled by Universal for a summer 1982 release, but the onslaught of such blockbusters as *E.T., Poltergeist* and *Star Trek II: The Wrath of Khan* (together with the failures of John Carpenter's *The Thing* and Ridley Scott's *Blade Runner*) caused it to be bumped forward—these self-luminous surfaces, though already ubiquitous, had not yet come in all shapes and sizes and were still part of an essentially analogue culture that was shared with such pre-electric media as photographs, magazines and billboards.

Nevertheless, as Vilem Flusser has remarked in his book *Post-History* (originally published in 1981), it was still surfaces and not texts that, by the early 1980s had already come to dominate our culture.[1] Drive-in theaters were still standing; movie theaters were still analogue, with their grainy, and highly tactile textures; and special effects were optically-based and done in-camera (although *Star Trek II* contains one of the first CGI images in film history when Kirk watches the unfolding of the Genesis planet on a video monitor: it is the seed of Post-Classic Cinema waiting to germinate two decades later)[2].

The television screen was based on cathode ray tube technology in 1983, and indeed, its presence is ubiquitous throughout *Videodrome*. There is scarcely a shot that exists without one, for television—together with its supplemental apparatuses of VCRs, videocassettes and cable TV—was *the* dominant medium of the 1980s. It had become what Marshall McLuhan, back in the mid-1960s had termed a "total surround," meaning an environment that is so pervasive as to become invisible to its inhabitants. "With the television image," as Jean Baudrillard remarks in his 1987 essay on "The Ecstasy of Communication," "—the television being the ultimate and perfect object for this new era—our own body and the whole surrounding universe become a control screen."[3]

Hence, *Videodrome* is a tale of a man who becomes swallowed up *inside* of a televisual reality, a subtle reality that is composed entirely out of electrons and photons because that is precisely what happened to Western consciousness during the 1980s. Our neurons had become so fused together with the electrons being sprayed at us via the cathode ray tube that there was simply no way of separating them anymore. Like Max Renn sticking his head inside the televisual mouth of radio personality Nicki Brand, we had been swallowed alive by it and were living on the inside of it, like Jonah in the whale's belly; there was no getting out. Electronic "encephalization" was Baudrillard's term for it.[4]

And soon an alchemical transformation began to take place, one that was documented in three great narratives of the early 1980s that envisioned this neuron-electron fusion which substituted images for facts in our brains: *Blade Runner* (1982), *Videodrome* (1983) and William Gibson's science fiction novel *Neuromancer* (1984). These are the three great narratives that captured the shift from textual lines to surfaces that Flusser spoke about, although it never occurred to Flusser that an over-saturation of such surfaces and their incandescent signifiers might cause paranoia, confusion and ontological disorientation in the psyches of unstable individuals not equipped with the right psychological immune systems for helping them to sort it all out.

Thus, the decade which demarcated this ontological transubstantiation in our collective psyche—an ontological shift in which phantoms slowly began to replace objects, things, facts, and indeed, even history itself (a process termed by Baudrillard "the precession of the simulacra," in which the simulacra began to *precede* and displace the real altogether[5])—began with two events: on December 8, 1980, Mark David Chapman murdered the icon named John Lennon by shooting him in the back with five bullets. For Chapman, Lennon did not exist as a real flesh and blood figure at all, but only as a mediatized saint whose image appeared on the "surfaces" of album covers, television talk shows like Dick Cavett and as a disembodied voice singing on LPs. Chapman sought to hunt down and kill Lennon because he didn't *really* believe that Lennon was anything more than a phantom to him until he lay dying on the pavement, blood leaking from his physical body right before his very eyes. Now he had proof at last that the mediatized phantom who had appeared on television was, in fact, a real person. Chapman had killed him. The proof lay right there on the sidewalk.[6]

The second event was the inauguration of Ronald Reagan on January 20, 1981. Reagan had been a former movie star and governor of California, but it soon became clear to the CIA and to his Cabinet members, that Reagan could not sit still for debriefings on public affairs without being shown *images*. After all, each morning Reagan would turn to the funnies in the newspaper first and scan their pictorial images before he moved on to glancing at the day's headlines. The CIA quickly realized that they had to debrief him in the form of making newsreel-style films for him to watch in order to capture his attention at all. And then, during his presidency, it became clear that Reagan couldn't remember for certain whether he had actually been in World War II or only played characters in World War II movies. He made several embarrassing public gaffes to this effect, and they can all be found in the biographies about him.

And then of course, John Hinckley, jr., modeling himself after Mark David Chapman, tried to assassinate Reagan on March 30th of that very same year because he was in love with a celluloid phantom: the thirteen year old prostitute named Iris who was played by Jodi Foster in Martin Scorsese's 1976 film *Taxi Driver*. Hinckley was certain that the act would impress the real Jodi Foster—in his case, at least, he knew there was a real person *behind* the phantom—enough to make her fall in love with him.[7]

Thus, the Age of Phantoms had begun, the age in which, as Flusser remarked, technical images (which are *post-alphabetic*) had come to replace historical events, because it is precisely writing—i.e. one-dimensional lines of text that seek to explain and decode two-dimensional images—that makes history possible (every scribe, as he puts it, is a demythologizer of images)[8] and this new culture of self-luminous images had begun to replace the brain's perception of things, objects and facts—the temporal procession of which actually makes up history—with phantasmatic images that had come to stand in for them.

For Baudrillard had already recognized three distinct historical orders of simulation: in the pre-modern epoch of first order simulation, the dominant paradigm is that of scene and mirror, as in Velazquez's painting *Las Meninas*: the representation reflects a real that is actually "out there" and is its faithful reflection and copy. But in the second order of simulation during the Industrial Revolution, the relation between the representation and the real begins to disintegrate since representations are now mass-produced and therefore begin to exhibit a problematic relation to the "original," from which, as Walter Benjamin argued, the aura is leeched by the copy.[9] Finally, in the postmodern epoch of third order simulation, the simulacra has nothing to represent, for it *precedes* the real, which no longer exists outside of the representation. There is only the hyperreal, or signs that signify other signs, but never refer to any kind of a real beyond them that they are supposed to represent. This is the precession, or precedence, of the simulacra over the real in the triumph of hyperreality.[10]

Now, Marshall McLuhan made a fundamental distinction in his 1962 book *The Gutenberg Galaxy* between media that function by means of "light through" them vs. media that operate in terms of requiring "light on" them. By the term "light through," McLuhan had in mind the cultural phenomena of the Medieval epoch, with its age of stained glass in which light irradiates colored glass to create self-luminous Biblical phantoms, but also things like illuminated manuscripts and the scribal art of "seeing through" a Biblical text using exegetical methods.[11] But with the shift to the invention of the printing press in the fifteenth century, the textural and highly tactile pages of illuminated manuscripts were traded out for the one-dimensional and uniform lines of type that required "light on" them in order to make them visible. The cosmology of saints and angels turning the etheric wheels of the heavens was traded out for that of Newtonian physics, in which matter was simply pushed and pulled about by external forces that required the light of the mind to illuminate the magical equations that made such forces possible.

The inception of the electric age, however, beginning with the telegraph and then evolving onwards through radio, radar and television screens, according to McLuhan, *retrieved* the cultural phenomenology of media that operate, once again—like stained glass—on the principle of "light through," rather than "light on" them. The visual bias that had been stepped *up* during the Renaissance was now in abeyance as the earlier Medieval biases of ear and hand—which he realized that Joyce had already foreseen in *Finnegans Wake* with his character of Humphrey Chimpden *Ear*wicker—were brought back into play. Jobs were traded out for roles, as the specialist was deprivileged over the generalist, for it was McLuhan's contention that both computer and television favored generalists. ("'Come into my parlor,' said the computer to the specialist" was one of his favorite aphorisms).[12] Hence, the eye—which scans rows of text one line at a time—was traded out for the ear, which hears everything all at once in a 360 degree radius.

McLuhan's distinction—as I have written about elsewhere[13]—can also be mapped onto a distinction made in ancient Hindu philosophy between two different types of material forms: those that compose the lower vibrational world of heavy, dense physical matter (which they termed *sthula*) and which require external light, such as the sun, to see them; and the forms of dream, myth and religion that are self-luminous and compose the higher vibrational realm of subtle matter (termed *sukshma*).[14] No external light is required to see them for they irradiate their own incandescence and, like video screens, are actually best seen in the dark.

In David Cronenberg's *Videodrome*—which is a visually poetic transform of McLuhan's ideas into narrative mode—the Videodrome signal erodes the cognitive ability of an individual to discern the difference between these two realms. Self-luminous phantoms made out of subtle matter— electrons and photons; hence McLuhan's "light through" phenomenon in which the television screen retrieves the mediatic effects of stained glass—invade the visual field of his waking reality where he is supposed to be able to survive amidst the clutter of the world of heavy matter, composed of the hard, unyielding atoms and molecules of Newtonian physics ("light on").

The psychological immune systems which Vilem Flusser overlooked as necessary for giving the individual a basis for discerning between this "plague of fantasies" (Slavoj Zizek's phrase)[15] and the Real that it overcoded, have to do, of course, with literacy and education. It was the Greek theoretician Cornelius Castoriadis who said that today, all anthropomorphic types—in past civilizations these were types like the thinker, the artist, the warrior—have been crushed into precisely *one* type, that of the consumer, while there has been a vast diminishment of all our "imaginary significations" to those which cluster about consumption. Imaginary significations, for Castoriadis, include a society's guiding *archai*: for the Greeks, this would've been things like the Greek gods and the guiding ideals of the democratic polis; for the Hebrews, it would've been Yahweh, together with all his commandments.[16] But with the "closure of signification" after WWII and the rise of the consumer as a single anthromorphic type, all dissent is crushed, and the signification process is closed. No one is encouraged to be critical of this consumerized consensus, and so no new meanings can emerge, since it is precisely through and by means of the tradition of the Greek agon, which involved a struggle between competing thinkers, that new meanings together with their significations are born.[17]

The individual, with the failure of our schools and the undermining of literacy with the rise of iconic culture, becomes as hapless as Plato's proverbial prisoner who mistakes the shadows on the wall cast by the firelight behind him for substance. Max Renn *is* that very figure who is held captive by the Videodrome signal that is beamed at him through the television screen that stands in for Plato's realm of phantoms and flickering shadows cast on the walls of the cave (what McLuhan would've called the "acoustic cavern of electric technology").[18] Renn never makes it out of the cave because he becomes more and more entranced and seduced by its images until his entire waking reality becomes the red room of the Videodrome stage without walls.

But Renn is, of course, a signifier—like Joyce's H.C.E.—who stands, as part for the whole, for us all today captured and dazzled by the spectacles of the video arena. The character of Truman in Peter Weir's 1998 film *The Truman Show*, unlike Renn, managed to escape from the cave of simulation and so Andrew Niccol's screenplay for that film comes much closer to the optimism of Plato's myth of the cave than David Cronenberg's narrative in *Videodrome*.[19] Niccol and Weir never tell us what Truman found beyond the stage set of the faux sky that his craft manages to poke a hole into, but Cronenberg's *Videodrome* suggests that we are all becoming irrevocably transformed—and dehumanized—by all these electronic images into something *else*, a New Flesh that has been physically and mentally altered beyond all recognition into something much more terrifying.

And with the ever-rising proliferation of spree killers making headlines daily, it seems that Cronenberg's film was more prescient than *The Truman Show*—which remains an ideal, but not a reality—while Cronenberg, back in 1983, held up the mirror to show us exactly where we were headed.

So here we are at last on the show called Videodrome, a strange new world in which we are going to have to learn how to survive. No Truman has yet arrived to show us the way out, but there are plenty of Max Renns who are being born into its New Flesh on an almost daily basis.

Thus, *Videodrome* remains *the* classic film dramatizing the fate of the psyche captured by what Jean Baudrillard called its "telemorphosis."[20] Information overload, paranoia and cognitive dissonance are its by-products, and we are seeing the end results of the replacement of history with post-historical surfaces unfolding, like Lennon dying on the sidewalk right in front of Chapman, before our very eyes.

Welcome to the video word made flesh.

This way to the arena.

"The circuit as such is a form that feeds back and feeds us into the circuit."
                                              --Marshall McLuhan

Opening Title Sequence
(0:00 – 3:14)

As the Universal logo comes onscreen, the ominous sounds of Howard Shore's synthesizer begin immediately, signaling to the viewer that he or she is about to enter, not a "brave new world," but an environment of anxiety, disorientation and threat. The title of the film, *Videodrome,* then appears in orange font as though it were being tuned in on a television screen that has just "unscrambled" some remote signal.

    The film's very first image, significantly, is that of a television screen playing a videocassette with the "Civic TV" logo that replicates itself in seven iterations of the primary colors. Beneath that, the logo reads: "Channel 83, Cable 12," informing us that this is no ordinary channel but an obscure cable television station. The grainy, low resolution lines that produce the image have been fired at the screen by a cathode ray tube that is rapidly scanning information in speed-of-light rows of electrons that transform the viewer himself into a projection screen. As Marshall McLuhan was fond of pointing out, the difference between a movie theater and a television is one of "light on" vs. "light through:" that is to say, that whereas the movie projector shines light upon a canvas, the television transforms the spectator himself into the screen across which the electrons project their image in a tactile way.[21] (Of course, this is no longer the case with LCD screens). Movies, like books, are visual, for they both require "light on" them to make them viewable; television, on the other hand, is tactile, for it gropes the viewer with electrons that interact with the brain's neurons to create what Deleuze and Guattari call "a machinic assemblage," or a human + television structural coupling.[22]

The little known German philosopher Gunther Anders—who came out of the Heidegger circle—insisted in his 1956 essay on television (entitled "The World as Phantom and as Matrix")[23] that television transformed the entire structure of the family household. For whereas the members of a traditional family once faced across the dinner table that was located in the center of the living room, where they could exchange glances and address each other directly, the television interrupted these human structural couplings when it displaced the family table as the center of the living room and caused everyone's heads to face in the same direction, transforming the living room into a miniature movie theater in which conversation became accidental. Thus, the television screen was the first electronic surface to begin the process of uncoupling humans from one another and creating new structural assemblages between the individual and his / her electronic interface with the matrix.

The next image played by the videocassette on Max Renn's television, appropriately, is a caricature of a man lying in bed with a television in his lap. Significantly, he is alone in the bed, clutching a teddy bear—since television, as Neil Postman pointed out in *The Disappearance of Childhood*,[24] also has an infantilizing effect on human society due to its erosion of the adult values configured by literacy—and so his relationship is not with another person, but with the television screen itself. An announcer's voice is then heard to inform the viewer that Civic TV is "the one you take to bed with you," implying that, since it is cable television and not one of the Big Three that once upon a time went off the air around 2 a.m., it is available for interface all night long. In a world of chronic human loneliness, the television provides small comfort as an exchange for social interaction.

The next image played by the videocassette—a sort of alarm clock, as it turns out—is that of a woman named Bridey James, the secretary of protagonist Max Renn, who now proclaims to Max that it is time to slowly, painfully ease himself back out of the dream world and into waking consciousness. She insists that *she* is not a dream—though she is, of course, an electronic phantom—and that she has arrived with his wake up call for Wednesday the 23rd to remind him that he has a meeting this morning at 6:30 a.m. with one Shinji Kuraki of Hiroshima Video.

The camera then pans back to reveal Max Renn's watch on his arm, splayed across the couch, with the time reading 5:30 a.m. Max has fallen asleep, alone, on the couch, implying that he has stayed up most of the night watching television by himself. He is soaked in a bluish pool of incandescent electrons as he begins to stir into wakefulness.

Max Renn's name is interesting to ponder for a moment since "Renn" suggests "Renaissance," or a "rebirth" of some kind, and indeed Max will be transformed by the end of the film into the Video Word Made Flesh. But "Renn" is also a homonym for "wren," the traditional king of all birds. On Saint Stephen's Day, December 26, a wren was killed because it was believed that the song of a wren betrayed Stephen's location when he was hiding and led to his death as the first Catholic martyr. And indeed, Max Renn will also become

Videodrome's first martyr. (Or at least its first test subject, as Brian O'Blivion later claims to have been its first victim).

In the next shot, Max proceeds to make himself an espresso and drink it while eating leftover pizza and looking at a series of large black and white photographs of the softcore porn that he is about to consider buying for his television station from Shinji Kuraki. He laughs at the naivete and modesty of the photographs and sets them aside, then dips his pizza crust into his espresso as he walks out of the frame.

Samurai Dreams
(3:15 – 6:00)

There follows an exterior shot of the run-down "Classic Hotel" where Max is supposed to meet with Shinji Kuraki and his associate. Max is then shown striding down the grimy, coffee-colored corridor of the hotel, where he knocks on one of its doors and Shinji Kuraki, a Japanese businessman wearing glasses and a plaid suit, inadvertently pulls open the door hard enough to yank the chain from its mooring on the wall in order to let Max in.

Max, seated at a table cluttered with liquor bottles and food wrappings that suggest the businessmen have been up drinking all night, then tells them that he's interested "a little bit" in the show and asks Shinji how many episodes he's got. Shinji replies that there are thirteen with the possibility of another six if the sales go well. Max asks him if he has videocassettes, and then Shinji laughs and tells him "of course," then signals to his partner, who is seated on a cheap sofa with cigarette burns in it, to open up the briefcase containing the cassettes. When he reaches for the cassette containing the first episode, Max stops him and insists that he show him only the last one, and when Shinji objects that they are arranged in chronological sequence, Max tells him that his audience most likely won't even see the first episodes.

Another televisual image then appears onscreen, showing a grainy, low-rez close-up shot of a sleeping geisha girl with the title "Samurai Dreams" appearing in pink lettering above her. The girl's eyes open abruptly, as though the urge to masturbate has just overcome her and she reaches for her dildo, which is costumed, bizarrely, in a miniature geisha outfit with a mask. She removes the costume from the dildo and begins to masturbate with it, but the shot is held from the waist up, so that only her bare breasts are visible as she does so. The material is not explicit enough for Max's cable television station.

Accordingly, the scene then transitions to a television set inside of Max Renn's office, where he sits watching the same cassette with his two business associates, Moses and Raphael. Max looks bored, a cigarette burning in his left hand as he scratches the temple of his forehead, and then asks his associates their opinion of the show. Moses opines that oriental sex is a natural and that it will bring Channel 83 an audience they've never had before, but Raphael, sitting directly across the conference table from Moses, tells Max that he doesn't think it's tacky enough. When Max asks him what he means by "tacky," Raphael tells him that it's just not tacky enough to turn him on and that too much class is bad for sex.

Max, stubbing out his cigarette, also voices doubts, muttering that he thinks it's too soft for what they're after. He wants something "tough," as he puts it, something that will "break through."

Cable television, though its origins go well back into the 1940s, was still a new medium, as far as a mass audience was concerned, in the early 1980s, and the scene points up the problem of what to do with a new medium. As McLuhan pointed out, new media come into being by swallowing up previous media: oral speech, for instance, became the content of the book just as the novel became the content of film, as film, in its turn, became the content of television.[25] YouTube originated in 2005 in order to provide a site for people to upload their cell phone footage of the 2004 Indian Ocean tsunami that killed 300,000 people.[26] Nobody at that point had any idea that absolutely *all* previous electric / electronic media—film, TV shows, commercials, music videos, etc.—would become the content of the new medium and create the current copyright controversies that now exist as a side effect of this "new media invasion."

In the early 1980s, MTV was just coming into being, and HBO and Showtime were attaining the first glimmerings of their mass popularity. Cable station programmers like Max Renn were scrambling about trying to find what they could play on their new stations, or even what kinds of stations could be invented for their new niche audiences.

Max, as it turns out, will *himself* become the content of the new medium of Videodrome, a special electronic signal that hi-jacks the brain's visual cortex and transforms its victims into human dream projectors who can no longer distinguish reality from their hallucinations. The Videodrome signal, that is to say, erodes the partition—whatever it is—that separates waking consciousness from dreaming consciousness, thereby transforming one's daylight hours into an endless surrealist landscape.

But this is, of course, metaphoric of the process of what theoretician Peter Sloterdijk calls "disinhibiting media,"[27] or those types of non-literate media—composed entirely of images, and especially violent images—that erode the inhibitions of individuals living in a civilized society who can no longer tell the difference between reality and mediatized fantasies, and tend to encourage a climate of ever proliferating spree killings, shootings and a general rise in violence amongst civilians supposedly sharing the same social order with each other.

In ancient Rome, the ever-increasing simulated violence in plays like those of Seneca's eventually led to the complete shut-down of the theaters in favor of the rise of the various hippodromes and gladiatorial arenas where the crowds preferred to see real violence enacted within zones of conflict specifically opened up within the zone of cooperation of the city of Rome itself. Violence became a spectacle sport to a crowd numbed by its brutality.

Today's hippodrome is indeed a "videodrome" as David Cronenberg calls it, a pulsating electromagnetic sheath that has surrounded the planet with global electronic technologies composed of molar aggregates of images of violence and pornography that the crowds seemingly prefer more and more often to any kind of "civilized" imagery at all.

Harlan
(6:01 – 9:04)

A tracking shot of the eroded rooftop of a building located somewhere in downtown Toronto now follows,[28] showing a satellite dish that is being adjusted to receive some distant electronic signal from the depths of outer space. The camera then follows the line of a cable connecting the dish to the sub-basement of the same building, where a technician named Harlan is busy working on a circuit board to unscramble the signal that is coming in from the dish. He is recording the information on a reel-to-reel player while Max, seated beside him looking at a catalogue of some sort, prompts him to play what he's got. Harlan then uses a screwdriver to make an adjustment on the circuitry as he informs Max that he has only managed to capture about 53 seconds of footage and that the other party's signal cut their pirating off with "an unscrambler scrambler."

Max then asks him what satellite the signal is coming from and Harlan tells him "Snooker," and when Max asks for country of origin, Harlan calculates that a 53 second delay must indicate that the signal is coming from somewhere in Malaysia.

Harlan, with his back turned to the monitor, then runs what he's captured on it for Max, who leans in to see a fuzzy image of a woman standing in front of an electrified red clay wall, to which she is being tied by two men wearing black hoods. After the men have secured her to the wall, they place a leather strap around her neck and begin choking her to death just as the image is washed out in a flood of gray interference patterns.

Max tells Harlan to hang a searcher on it next time, and Harlan says that he's already at work on it, and then asks Max whether he's interested. Max gives forth an indifferent "yeah" and then tells Harlan to do something about the signs he's made which say, "This Way to Video Boutique." He points out that after all they're supposed to be running a clandestine operation (since they are essentially stealing programs from all over the globe, as their operation is too small to afford to buy any rights to the programs). They are video pirates on the high frequency seas, as another of Harlan's signs indicates.

Such telecommunications satellites were put into orbit around the earth in the early 1960s by Hughes Air—Syncom 2 was launched in July of 1963, which relayed the first satellite telephone call between President Kennedy and Abubakr Balewa, the Nigerian prime minister—and they had the effect of wrapping the planet inside of an invisible cocoon of electromagnetic signals beaming the images of dead celebrities, old television reruns and radio broadcasts across its entire surface.[29] This was a technologized retrieval of the ancient Ptolemaic cosmology which imagined the earth to be encased inside of a series of whirling etheric spheres containing not only each one of the seven heavenly bodies, but also angels, archons and the disembodied spirits of saints. The satellization of the planet in the 1960s represented the beginnings of what has currently evolved into the complete dematerialization of technology, which, as the decades have gone by ever since, has slowly become more and more removed from its material substrates.

Such distance annihilating technologies, furthermore—as Heidegger was the first to point out—have the effect of making the far near and the near far, and thus of rendering the very concept of "place" obsolete.[30] When no particular place is any more privileged than any other, the planet becomes a rhizome of homogenized parking lots, shopping malls and video monitors. It is all quantitatively the same value-neutral plane of deworlded horizons and empty cartographical vectors. Any truck stop café, as McLuhan put it, with a newspaper and a television becomes as cosmopolitan as New York or Paris.[31] Special sites for the occurrence of theophanies—the Mount of Olives, the Rock of the Dome, the cave where this or that saint once dwelled—can, in such a value-neutral world, no longer exist. Sacred geography simply becomes relegated to the status of an archaism.[32]

The image that Harlan manages to extract from this electromagnetic shell is one of torture and brutality that is completely deterritorialized from plot, narrative or story conventions of any kind, for in the electronic world of instantaneity, such conventions are also rendered obsolete. The distancing of violence in remote Third World countries is simply dissolved when such signals can be captured by electronic apparatuses that are capable of installing them into the living rooms of the average suburban household.

The 53 second clip of the woman being tortured by men wearing black hoods, furthermore, bears a certain resemblance to the videos of black-hooded terrorists broadcast nowadays by the media on an almost daily basis, for the terrorist, as Boris Groys has pointed out, has appropriated all the media of the contemporary artist: film, TV, video, etc.[33] And because all the terrorist need do is punch a button activating a bomb somewhere for his deeds to become immediately circulated around the globe via the mass media, he has rendered the contemporary artist obsolete as a producer of shocking images. It is the terrorist, not the artist, nowadays, who captures the public imagination with vivid, unforgettable images circulated through the global "videodrome." The public imagination is no longer captivated by Mona Lisas, Michelangelo sculptures or drip paintings, but rather by collapsing buildings, burning hotels, and bombs going off everywhere. Art, under such conditions, has become superfluous.[34]

It is now such images of violence and mayhem that are beamed at the public spectator via satellite or YouTube upload that shock and worry him, as the distance annihilating powers of modern electronic technologies send one civilization crashing into another. These are the darker implications of McLuhan's Global Village, in which electronic technologies have shrunk the earth down to the size of a small village and everyone is now involved in everyone else's business. Privacy, under such conditions, is also a thing of the past.

And those images of pure violence, deterritorialized from any narratives, feed back into the public mind, where they contribute to the erosion of inhibitions and inspire the discontented among us to enact such images in real life.

The Word—or today we should say, the Image—comes first: *then* the Flesh.

The Rena King Show
(9:05 – 12:04)

The next scene takes place in a television studio, where Max Renn is seated in one of the guest chairs of The Rena King Show. He is nervously lighting up a cigarette as he turns to the show's other live guest, pop psychologist Nicki Brand, and asks her if she wants a smoke. When the camera pans over to her, however, it first glimpses her through the continuous feed of a video monitor, where she is wearing a red dress and seated in front of a fake potted palm. Nicki declines the cigarette and a wide shot then follows which reveals the entire stage of the show: a make-up man is busy putting the final touches on Rena King's face, who sits to the left of a television set upon which media prophet Brian O'Blivion (Cronenberg's stand-in for Marshall McLuhan) waits patiently to be interviewed. On the back-drop behind them, the theme of the show reads: "Television and Social Responsibility."

The shot cuts once again back to a monitor as the show's announcer comes on to introduce The Rena King Show, whose guests include Max Renn, controversial president of Channel 83; radio personality Nicki Brand and media prophet professor Brian O'Blivion.

Rena's first question is directed at Max: she wants to know why his cable television station offers everything from soft core pornography to graphic violence to its viewers.

Max, shifting back and forth in his chair, explains to her that it's merely a matter of economics and that his station is small and so in order to survive, it must provide the public something they can't get anywhere else.

But Rena wonders whether such shows contribute to a climate of social violence and sexual malaise and asks Max whether he cares or not.

Max replies by saying that he certainly does care, and that he cares enough in fact to give his viewers a harmless outlet for their fantasies. Max insists that what he's doing is a socially positive act.

Rena then turns to Nicki Brand and asks her whether she thinks what Max is doing is socially positive.

Nicki says that society lives in over stimulated times and that it craves stimulation for its own sake. She insists that it always wants more and more, whether it's emotional, tactile or sexual and that she thinks this is bad.

But Max interrupts and asks her why she is wearing that red dress. He insists that Freud would've had something to say about her dress, but Nicki doesn't deny it. She admits that she lives in a constant state of sexual excitation.

Max, turned on, leans over and tells her that he'd like to take her out to dinner.

Rena, flustered that her show is becoming a performance of the very theme she is seeking to take a critical stance toward, then turns to the television set on the stage and addresses Professor O'Blivion, asking him whether he thinks erotic and violent television shows lead to social desensitization.

O'Blivion then puzzles Rena—as McLuhan was so fond of doing on talk shows—with an aphorism, as he says that television has become the retina of the mind's eye and that this is why he refuses to appear on television except *on* a television (nowadays, of course, he would be appearing via Skype). He further elaborates that "O'Blivion" is not the name he was born with, but rather his television name and that soon everyone will have special names designed to cause the cathode ray tube to "resonate."

Rena has no idea how to respond to such media koans, so she turns back to Nicki in order to ask her whether she thinks Max Renn is a menace to society. Nicki tells her that she's not sure about that but he is certainly a menace to *her*.

Now the interesting thing about this scene is not so much its "content," i.e. the discussion about the dehumanizing effects of violent and sexual imagery upon society (since that topic is the very theme explored by the film), but rather its media semiotics. Max Renn, to begin with, as a guest on a television talk show has now become the *content* of television, just as he will later become the content of the Videodrome signal that will erode his ability to discern the Real from the Imaginary orders. He has now been put *inside* of television and the continuous pick-up of the TV cameras—like that of a microphone—strips a dematerialized avatar away from him and sends it beaming at the speed of light into the various television homes throughout Toronto which are tuned in to The Rena King Show.

Notice that the first time the viewer sees Nicki Brand, she appears as her two-dimensional avatar on a video monitor, wearing a red dress—traditionally the color of the spilled blood of Christ, the sacrificial Lamb in the Catholic church—thus foreshadowing her later fate as sacrificial lamb to the Videodrome show, where she is murdered and thus robbed of her three-dimensional flesh and blood body, leaving behind only her two-dimensional avatar within the Videodrome matrix. She will play the role of a sort of Videodrome Muse to Max Renn, whom she will seduce into its power to transform by means of the dematerialization process of removing images from their material substrates, which is precisely what our current electronic technologies have been doing to us for decades.

Professor O'Blivion, too—as we later find out—can only appear in avataric form on television because he is already dead, killed by a brain tumor. His daughter simply books him as a guest on talk shows by playing cassettes of his monologues, which perhaps explains why his answers to Rena's questions are so puzzlingly evasive. He has already achieved the status of a pure dematerialized icon whose physical substrate has long since disappeared from the world.

So, just as McLuhan told us to pay attention to the medium and not the message, it becomes clear that The Rena King Show's thematic discussion of the dehumanizing effects of violent images upon society is beside the point, for the point is the power of these electric / electronic media to create ghosts and avatars through the very process of etherealization that historically, once upon a time, led to the creation of icons of saints and religious figures who had likewise long since disappeared from the world, leaving behind only their ghostly images in the various media of fresco, canvas and paint.[35]

Of course, the whole purpose of Modernist Art beginning with Malevich and his white and black squares was to provide a critique of the image, which, down to the canvases of Pollock and Rothko, led to its complete dismantling and disappearance. Popular culture, on the other hand, has been iconphilic all along, and so it has retained for itself—as Modernist Art and some contemporary art have not—the right to propagate shocking images, a right, however, as remarked above, that has lately been stolen from it by the terrorist with his global media apparatus.[36]

Thus, the *real* subtext of The Rena King Show involves the iconophilic power of the Culture Industry and its ability to create an Imaginary Order that is so packed with powerful images that it has tempted even a traditionally iconphobic religion as Islam to want to appropriate its technical apparatus for the production of their own shocking icons, icons such as beheadings and burning buildings which, as Professor O'Blivion would say, cause the cathode ray tube to "resonate."

Pittsburgh
(12:05 – 13:16)

The next shot transitions to the video monitor in Harlan's sub-basement, where Max is watching a longer Videodrome sequence of a man hanging from the ceiling by manacles tying up his arms. The scene takes place in the same red room with a black rubber mat on the floor as the earlier 53 second clip, while two hooded men electrocute their victim with some sort of electrified gadget. Max asks Harlan, who is busy working on equipment behind him, when the plot of the show is supposed to unfold, but Harlan informs him that there is no plot and that the show goes on like that for an hour of torture, murder and mutilation. Max marvels at the brilliance of the show, since there are almost no production costs and it seems incredibly realistic. He wonders where actors could be found that could do such work and he asks Harlan whether he had trouble locking onto the signal this time. Harlan tells him that he didn't, since he realized the Malaysia delay was a plant and that the Prince of Pirates cannot be fooled for long. Max, growing impatient, demands to know where the signal is coming from and Harlan tells him, simply: Pittsburgh. Max, incredulous, echoes back at him: *Pittsburgh*?

Thus, what Max had thought to be an image of the torture of political prisoners in some far distant Third World country turns out to be imagery that is being generated across the Canadian border in the United States. The point of origin of the Videodrome signal is creeping closer and closer to Max Renn's cable television office in Toronto. Indeed, as he is watching the image unfold—an image which Harlan never looks at—the Videodrome signal is slowly seeping into his brain and actually transforming its very architecture. Soon he will himself become the source of his own Videodrome signal, a receiver no longer but rather a transmitter of hallucinations of sex and violence that destroy his ontological ability to discern reality from fantasy, as his sense of identity disintegrates. Indeed, as McLuhan once remarked: "Pornography and violence are by-products of societies in which private identity has been…destroyed by sudden environmental change."[37]

Of course, later he will learn that the Videodrome signal is even closer than Pittsburgh, and that it is actually coming from within Toronto itself, from a company called Spectacular Optical which has chosen his cable TV station as the intended host by means of which to broadcast their signal. It is a Pentecostal image: instead of the Logos descending into all the minds of the apostles to confer on them the various languages necessary for disseminating the Gospel, Channel 83 will become the means for propagating the electronic Word that will enter through every television set in Toronto to transform the architecture of the minds of everyone who watches it into Videodrome apostles of the living Image made Flesh. And instead of disciples spreading the Word like a virus to all who are ready to open their mouths and receive its communion, the disciples of Videodrome will set forth, guns in their hands, to spread the malaise of spree killings throughout the city.

Nicki Brand
(13:16 – 18:43)

In the next scene, Max is shown striding up the steps to an upper floor of the CRAM radio station where, in a tiny studio behind an oval pane of glass, Nicki Brand is on the line with a caller. Max watches her through the window as she talks a distressed caller through her problems with her sister. Nicki urges the caller to phone their Distress Center. The caller then hangs up and the show's announcer informs the audience that they will return to Nicki Brand and the Emotional Rescue Show in a moment.

In the next shot, Nicki and Max are back at his shadowy apartment. Nicki, while flipping through a cardboard box of videocassettes on the floor, asks Max whether he's got any porno. Max is making them drinks and he asks Nicki whether she's really serious. She tells him that it gets her in the mood, and then she finds a tape in the box labeled "Videodrome." When she asks Max what it is, he tells her off-handedly that it concerns torture, murder, etc., and she says that it sounds great and slides the cassette into the VCR before Max even has a chance to object. He tells her that it ain't exactly sex, to which she replies: "Says who?"

As they both seat themselves on Max's sofa, the snowy image on the television screen reads "Videodrome" in the same orange font that was tuned in for the movie's title sequence. When the picture comes on, a naked young Asian girl, tied to the red clay wall, is being flogged with a whip by another black-hooded man.

Nicki says that she can't believe what she's seeing and when Max, momentarily relieved, offers to turn it off, she insists that she wants to watch it. She asks whether he can get the image any clearer but he tells her that it's a pirate tape that's been scrambled. Nicki insists that it turns her on and suggests that Max get out his Swiss army knife and cut her with it on her shoulder, just a little. When he examines her left shoulder and sees a series of slashes, he says that it looks as though someone has already beaten him to it.

Nicki wonders aloud how one gets to be a contestant on Videodrome, and Max replies that he doesn't know since nobody ever seems to come back the following week. Distracted, he asks her to clarify what happened to her shoulder and examines the markings again. She tells him that it was a "friend" who she thinks would also like Videodrome.

Max, incredulous, says, "You mean you let somebody cut you?"

Nicki nods pleasantly, smiling, and asks Max if he'd like to try a few things with her.

In the next shot, the camera floats across Max's living room to reveal the two of them lying on a blanket that they have spread out on the floor in front of the television, where the Videodrome tape cassette is still playing. They are both naked and Max appears to be entering her from the rear as he takes a long hatpin and slowly punches it through her earlobe as she moans with *jouissance*. He carefully pulls it out and licks the blood from it. Then he turns her over to face him, kisses her and plunges the needle through her other earlobe, where he leaves it in as he kisses her once again, more fiercely this time.

As he enters her in the missionary position, the camera pulls back to reveal that the couple are now on the same ribbed black rubber mat that the viewer has so far seen only on the Videodrome tapes. As the shot continues to widen, the two figures are revealed to be entwined on the mat like something out of a Francis Bacon painting, and the familiar red clay wall of the Videodrome room now becomes visible behind them. The entire room is red, and there are four pillars supporting the ceiling, pillars that are adorned with various torture racks and their implements. The sound of Nicki's moans of pleasure become louder and louder until they melt with Howard Shore's sinister-sounding synthesizer.

Both Max and Nicki, by this point, have been exposed to the brain-altering Videodrome signal, and the final image of this scene is metaphoric of the fact that both of them have now become the *content* of Videodrome. They are no longer spectators but actors within the "video arena," for their neurons have been saturated with cathode ray electrons that function to create a neural-electronic assemblage between the two humans and the electronic signal.

The television, that is to say, is not just some neutral gadget that "depends upon how you use it." Its screen is composed of a series of rigidly parallel lines that act as neural disruptors opening up the neurons to become receptive to images of sex and violence that are then fed into the brain's visual cortex where it can be manipulated. The fact that watching images of torture turns Nicki on and makes her want to enact S&M on the physical plane signifies that mediatized images are not at all harmless, but rather feed back into the Real from the Imaginary Order. Those images, once they arrive inside the brain's visual cortex, function as little pods of destruction waiting to be enacted on the plane of materiality, depending, of course, upon the degree to which the particular individual exposed is receptive to such images.

Like food commercials or pornography itself, violence can indeed function as a kind of porn with the potentiality—although not the certainty—of being realized within the arena of actuality.

As Plato well knew, in the beginning was the Image, not the Word, for images and ideas precede their incarnation on the material plane. This is also the point made by Deleuze in *Difference and Repetition* when he says that virtual Ideas incarnate themselves as extensities (i.e. physical matter) by means of intensities (flows, gradients, vectors, etc.).[38]

Indeed, the electroverse is a gigantic Body without Organs that uses humans as multiplicities arranged upon it as its organs.[39]

Both Max and Nicki, then, have now become organs upon the BwO of Videodrome.

Masha
(18:44 – 21:23)

There follows an exterior morning shot of downtown Toronto with its gleaming metallic skyscrapers. The camera then pans down to the Civic TV offices as Max enters the building, weary and hungover from the night before. He walks down the central corridor which is lined with movie posters, passing a cameraman on his way to his secretary's office. Bridey, with a cigarette in one hand and a cup of coffee in the other, greets him from behind the desk and tells him that Masha Borowczyk has been waiting in his office for over an hour to see him. He tells her he doesn't think he's ready for a meeting with Masha, but she thrusts the cigarette into his left hand and the cup of coffee into his right hand and tells him, "Masha, go. She's hot to trot."

In the next scene, yet another television is featured, this one in Max's office, while the voice of Masha, with its Eastern European accent, informs him that the show she is offering him for sale is called *Apollo and Dionysus*. But Max, bored, fast forwards through a series of images of bare-breasted women and men in togas pouring wine and conversing with each other. Max asks Masha whether the show ever gets good. Sitting across from him at the conference table and wearing a fake leopard skin jacket—she is an older woman—she insists that it is *all* good, but he tells her candidly that it's not what he's looking for. He wants something a bit more…contemporary. Moving to the chair right beside her, he explains that he wants something that will show people what's *really* going on beneath the sheets. He insists that *Apollo and Dionysus* is too naïve for his market, too sweet. Like her.

He shuts off the tape and she concedes that it's *his* market. Then he asks her if she's ever heard of a show called "Videodrome," and she obviously hasn't so he spells the word "drome" out for her and explains that it means "video circus, video arena" and that it's just torture and murder without plot or characters and is extremely realistic. He tells her that he thinks "it's what's next."

"Then God help us," she comments.

"Better on TV than on the streets," he replies and offers her the commission if she can track it down for him, to which she agrees.

After ejecting the cassette from the VCR, she asks him whether he's ever considered producing his own show right in the building and he explains that it's not the type of thing he has the temperament to do. But she asks him to hypothesize, if he *did* have the temperament, what type of show would he do? Videodrome?

The irony of Masha's question is that Max, without knowing it, has already become the "star" of the live action TV show called *Videodrome*. He has already become its first test subject and is being carefully observed by the show's executives—including Harlan, whom he thinks is working for him—to see how the saturation of his brain's neurons with the Videodrome signal will cause him to behave.

Jean Baudrillard termed the process of the gradual swallowing up of the Real by so-called "reality television shows" the "telemorphosis" of the banal. The engulfing of reality by the screen is the "perfect crime," as he puts it, for it leaves no traces: even the accomplices of Truman in *The Truman Show* are equally telemorphosized along with him, as we all are nowadays.[40]

But David Cronenberg, back in 1983, long before the advent of reality television, already foresaw that the content of television would soon shift from the studios to the streets. Hence, the other irony of this scene when Max says, "Better on TV than on the streets," for he is already becoming the guinea pig in the new experiment of Videodrome that is attempting to transform his life—a generation ahead of Truman's—into a television show in which violence and sex are deterritorialized from all narrative content whatsoever. The Videodrome signal is metaphoric of the complete saturation and surrounding of public space by the ubiquitous camera eye that transforms banality into a spectacle without spectators, only actors.[41]

Cigarette Burn
(21:24 – 23:49)

Inside the blue and brown gloom of Max's apartment, he and Nicki are resting in post-coital mode. Max is sitting with his back to the couch, head propped up on a throw pillow, cigarette dangling from his left hand as Nicki informs him that she is going away the next day on assignment for two weeks. She tells him to guess where she's going and he suggests, flippantly, "L.A.?" But she tells him she's going to Pittsburgh and he makes a joke about not staying in the sun too long as he hears it's bad for the skin.

Nicki, seated on the couch in black bra and panties, is adjusting her make-up with a compact when she reminds him that Pittsburgh is where Videodrome is made and that she intends to audition for the show. She insists that she was made for that show, to which Max replies that nobody on earth could be made for *that* show.

But then, suddenly alarmed by her recklessness, he stubs out his cigarette and grabs the compact away from her, insisting that he listen to her. He tells her to stay *away* from Videodrome, as such mondo weirdo video guys have unsavory connections and they play rough, rougher than even Nicki Brand can play.

She merely smiles at his agitation and says that it sounds like a challenge. As Max collapses back onto the couch, defeated, she asks for a cigarette and he fishes one out and lights it for her, explaining to her that in countries like Brazil and Central America, the making of underground video is considered a subversive act for which people are executed. In Pittsburgh…who knows?

Nicki takes the lit cigarette, drags on it and then lies back on the couch. While Max is busy pouring more liquor, she signals for his attention, drags on the cigarette and then, to his dismay, burns a tiny round wound with it onto her right breast just above the black lace of her bra. She seems to enjoy the pain, however, and hands the cigarette back to Max who continues to insist that she not audition for Videodrome.

But it is the last time he will ever see her in the realm of physical materiality again.

The aptly named "Nicki Brand"—whose last name suggests both "brand" as in "branding iron" and "brand" as in "brand name"—will soon, like a dead celebrity, disappear from the physical world to be reconstituted as an electronic phantom. Her red blood cells will be transubstantiated into electrons, for whenever Max sees her from henceforth, she will only appear as a cathode ray image. She will become a sort of iconic muse for Videodrome, the vaginal port of entry through which he will enter bodily, to be telemorphosized by its signal.

McLuhan said that the difficult thing to grasp about television is that it is primarily a tactile medium due to its reversal of the traditional role of screen and spectator.[42] The spectator becomes the screen as the electrons pour across him, altering the way his brain processes information. But if the television screen is tactile, it is also most assuredly iconophilic, for it transforms dead celebrities into eternal avatars composed of its relentlessly scanning rows of crackling electrons.

Pittsburgh, incidentally, was where Andy Warhol grew up, that master painter of modern celebrity icons, and so it is appropriate that—though it is later revealed that Videodrome does *not* stem from Pittsburgh—it is referenced as the place where Nicki thinks she is headed in order to audition for Videdrome, for the sinister men who run Videodrome will indeed murder her and transform her into its central iconic Muse in order to lure Max more fully into its matrix.[43]

Max and Masha
(23:50 – 27:22)

The next scene takes place in a Greek restaurant as Max and Masha Borowczyk watch a belly dancer moving to the rhythms of a bouzouki. The belly dancer descends a staircase past their table as Masha lights up a Turkish cigarette which uncomfortably reminds Max of the previous night with Nicki. Masha notices his discomfort and asks whether he has a hangover but he tells her he only stayed up late watching TV. But then he gets directly to the point and asks Masha whether she has managed to get in touch with "their friends" in Pittsburgh. She tells him that she did, in a way, through the subterranean grapevine. She then warns him that Videodrome is dangerous and that it is something for him to leave alone (although Max has already been captured by the signal that is working its way into the deeper recesses of his brain).

Masha insists that Videodrome is not for public consumption but Max counters by saying that Channel 83 is a little too small to be considered public. She says that, even so, it is still too public, but he wants to know why. She simply tells him that it's dangerous and he hypothesizes that if it's Mafia-run, then they can be convinced to do business, but she corrects him by saying that it is more…*political* than that.

Max presses her for further clarification and she tells him that the images on Videodrome are not fake but real: it's a form of snuff TV. Max doesn't believe it. He insists that it's safer and cheaper to fake such violent images. However, she tells him that Videodrome has something he doesn't have: a philosophy. And *that* is what makes it dangerous.

When he demands to know *whose* philosophy is involved, she is evasive, but he wants a name, even promising that they can take a shower together sometime. She tells him that she's sure he would be very beautiful but that she prefers younger men, and flirts with the young peroxide blonde waiter that brings her coffee to the table.

Max then reiterates: he wants a name. He even offers to make *Apollo & Dionysus* part of the package. She tells him that that hurts her, and he says, "Hey, the world's a shithole, ain't it?"

Charmed by his cynicism, she relents and gives him the name: Professor Brian O'Blivion.

Now, Brian O'Blivion, as I have remarked above—who has only appeared thus far in avataric form on a television screen on The Rena King Show—is Cronenberg's stand-in for Marshall McLuhan, the Toronto genius who, together with Harold Innis, originated the field of media studies back in the 1950s.[44] The primary difference between McLuhan and his caricature, however, is that whereas McLuhan was a literary man and writer of many books, O'Blivion seems to have been primarily a video artist, for we will soon discover that he has made shelves and shelves of video tapes of himself monologuing on various aspects of media.

O'Blivion, as will also be revealed, originated the idea for Videodrome and sold it to a corporation called Spectacular Optical who may, or may not, have had him murdered. O'Blivion, like McLuhan, is Catholic, and his appropriation of the metaphysical vulva[45] to give birth to the modern incarnation of the Logos as an electronic signal capable of transforming the architecture of the brain from a merely passive receiver of televised images to a transmitter of them into physical space is a classic McLuhanesque reversal of an overheated medium. The televisual spectator is normally in a passive role and simply receives the images that are then played upon its screen into his psyche, where they act as neural disruptors to manipulate him into going out and buying and consuming its advertised products. But the Videodrome signal reverses the equation, for Max Renn is already becoming a human cathode ray tube who will soon be projecting such socially disruptive images, as Rena King called them, into three dimensional physical space, thereby transforming him from a receiver of a signal to a transmitter. Thus, the Shannon-Weaver model, which McLuhan criticized for not taking the bias of the medium transmitting the signal into account, is reversed.[46]

Eventually, Max will be recoded to become an assassin for the Videodrome executives who wish to take over his cable television station, and so the question raised by Cronenberg is: to what degree do electronic media isolate and cut off the individual from society? Can a human being living under the conditions of complete electronic saturation maintain his existence as a social animal or not?

Or is the real truth rather that all these "new media" capture and isolate the individual consciousness into forming a human + screen assemblage that renders all other human relations peripheral to the loop—as is suggested by Lawrence Pearce's cover design for the present book, in which the "encephalization" of Max Renn by the Accumicon has the effect of cutting him off into a private world of video hallucinations that do not feed back into any sort of real at all, but only an electromagnetic matrix without ground.

The questions raised by *Videodrome* in 1983 are more relevant now than ever, since everywhere one looks—riding on buses, driving in cars, watching movies in theaters—all one sees is a constant array of tiny, self-luminous screens capturing the attention of the user to the exclusion of everyone else around him or her.

(The spree killer would seem to constitute a sort of social attempt to disrupt this feedback loop between screen and user by insisting upon the fact, rather violently, that he has been cut out of the loop and demands attention from the very social order that is ignoring him).

Cathode Ray Mission
(27:23 – 31:39)

The next scene features Max walking past the exterior wall of an old gray building covered with tattered handbills as he maneuvers through a line of derelicts and homeless people filing up the steps of the building where a blue and red sign reads: "Cathode Ray Mission."[47]

The noisy room inside has been divided by a series of partitions into graffiti covered cubicles, each one of which features a desk with a small black and white television affixed to it, where a derelict is seated watching the screen indifferently. Max files through this chaos looking for a figure who might convey some sort of authority over it all. He pauses a moment to peer above one of the partitions where he sees a hatted man with dirty brown gloves watching a black and white television that has been chained to the cubicle. The man looks up at him and gives a crooked smile.

Max continues moving past the cubicles until he rounds a corner where he spots who he's looking for: a conservatively dressed woman with her auburn hair pulled back in a tight bun giving directions to the staff. She notices him as he makes his way past her to the roped stairwell leading to the second floor and so turns to follow him.

"Bianca O'Blivion?" he inquires.

As she unhooks the rope and says, "Yes," he then introduces himself and explains to her that he was on a panel show with her father, The Rena King Show. She remembers the show and says that he said some very superficial things about violence, sex and catharsis. When she asks him what he wants, he hooks the rope back to its latch behind them and says that he wishes to speak to her father about a new twist in video that he may not be aware of.

In the next shot, Max and Bianca are shown entering Brian O'Blivion's office: a dark and cluttered study with shelves of antique volumes, sketches of Christ at the various Stations of the Cross, Medieval tapestries and chairs, a statue of the angel Gabriel blowing his horn at the Apocalypse, and portrait busts of ecclesiastical figures. Max peers through the heavy curtains where a window overlooks the floor of partitions and cubicles below. He comments, sardonically, that he loves the view.

Bianca tells him that he looks like one of her father's derelicts, to which Max jokingly replies that he thinks it's a style that's coming back. But Bianca, severe and grim, tells him that in their case it's not a style but rather a disease forced on them by lack of access to the cathode ray tube.

She is standing at her father's desk where a metallic-looking chair sits empty, while behind it has been hung a huge Renaissance tapestry depicting some Biblical scene. A statue of a figure resembling Moses overlooks the scene from one corner, while near him two tall, ornate candlesticks with burning white candles inscribe their shadows onto the wall behind them.

Max, standing near a table arranged with a collection of small statues, asks her whether she really thinks a few doses of TV are going to help those derelicts?

Bianca replies by insisting that watching TV will help patch them back into the world's mixing board. Max gives forth an ironic "Absolutely." But noticing the video camera in the corner, he asks Bianca if she encourages her father's derelicts to make home movies?

She responds by saying that Professor O'Blivion sends "video letters" all over the world.

When Max then asks whether the professor is available, Bianca tells him that she is her father's screen, and that once he's informed her of the purpose of his visit, her father may wish to send him a cassette in reply. Which format would he prefer?

Max tells her that that will make conversation a little difficult, but Bianca explains that her father has not engaged in conversation for over twenty years. The monologue is his preferred mode of discourse—as it was McLuhan's, whether he was being interviewed or not—and when she asks, once again, which format he would prefer, Max says, "Videodrome." Bianca pretends not to know what he's talking about and asks him if that is a Japanese configuration.

Max, astonished that she's never heard of it, informs her that there have been some serious gaps in her education. He insists that she mention "Videodrome" to her father and that he may want to have a conversation with Max when he hears about it. He then stands up from the red-upholstered antique chair and turns to leave. Pausing once more to gesture vaguely at the entire study, he tells her that he "loves the view."

Marshall McLuhan was a Catholic who, as a professor, had a particular interest in the Medieval epoch. *The*

Gutenberg Galaxy (1962), one of his most famous books, focused on how the rise of the printing press in the fifteenth and sixteenth centuries completely dismantled the structures of the Medieval age with the rise of the printed book, mass literacy, and the concept of the private scholar. He connected the rise of literacy with the shift in art from pre-perspectival to three-dimensional perspectival space, and he insisted that these mediatic shifts favored the sense of sight above the Medieval audile-tactile sense ratios, in which space and time are discontinuous.[48] Each object, saint or religious figure in a Medieval work of art *makes* its own space and so there is no privileged point of view: the subject with a private point of view to which—whether in a book or in a painting—he subjects all other spaces and times was an invention of the Gutenbergian era.

But in the present scene of *Videodrome*, David Cronenberg transforms McLuhan's Catholicism and technophobia into Brian O'Blivion's creation, not only of the Videodrome idea itself, but of the surreal Cathode Ray Mission where, instead of the derelict being fed the Word of God and taken up through the liturgy of the mass into the mystical body of Christ, he is instead given the Word-made-electron and taken up into the photonic matrix, a vast cyberspace in which electrons and neurons become entwined. The spray of electrons through the dilated pupil of the eye thus takes the place of the communion wafer that enters in through the mouth to gather the wayward soul up into the Body of the Matrix.

Thus, whereas McLuhan was critical and skeptical of technology ("I am resolutely opposed to all innovation, all change," he has been quoted as saying)—insisting that one could only escape from being manipulated by media through understanding how it functions[49]—Brian O'Blivion is a technophile who makes use of video cameras, cassettes and televisions to propagate his "letters to the world."

And as the inventor of Videodrome, he is indeed its metaphysical father.

The Videocassette
(31:40 – 38:55)

In the next scene, Max Renn is seated at the coffee table in front of his couch, making a series of calculations as he flips through sheets of paper, cigarette in hand, while the endless scenes of torture that compose Videodrome play on his television in the corner beneath his drawn Venetian blinds. Voices echo through his head: Harlan's, Masha's, Nicki's. He hears Masha's voice in particular telling him that "Videodrome has a philosophy and that is what makes it dangerous."

In the next shot, he is at the kitchen counter shown unzipping a black triangular case containing a gun, a Walther PPK, but we are not told where the gun has come from. The novelization of the film written by Jack Martin (a pseudonym for horror fiction writer Dennis Etchison) however, based as such novelizations usually are on an earlier draft of the screenplay, informs us that he went inside the closet of his bedroom and found the gun, which had been given to him once upon a time by someone named "Deborah," with an inscription in gold lettering that reads: "For Max, who can't resist shooting his mouth off. With love from Deborah."[50]

The novelization also hints that he went to dig the gun out because he felt that for some obscure reason he would need to use it.

In the present scene of the movie, Max unwraps the gun from its brown paper and turns it clumsily over in his hands, inadvertently causing the clip to fall out. He obviously has no idea how to use the weapon, but at that moment there comes a knock at his door and so he quickly scrambles to hide the gun under a newspaper on the counter, then goes to answer the front door.

His secretary Bridey charges in, telling him that she has brought his wake-up cassette and something else that came to the office for him by courier. But he is anxious to know the fate of Nicki and he asks Bridey if she was able to find anything out about her "assignment" at CRAM. Bridey tells him that CRAM said that Nicki was *not* on assignment but that she had a month off coming to her and so she decided to take it now.

As Bridey attempts to insert a videocassette into his VCR, Max yells at her not to touch it and runs across the room and violently slaps her face, which for a moment he sees as Nicki Brand. He then slaps her again, and she reverts back to Bridey, who tells him that he scared her.

When she asks what is wrong with him, he scratches his belly and tells her he doesn't know but that he feels like he might be getting a rash or something. When he apologizes for hitting her, she looks puzzled and says that he didn't hit her. He quickly backpedals and says that of course he didn't hit her, stumbling over what to say next, for he is as confused as she is.

When she offers to stay and look after him he quickly ushers her out the door, explaining that he was in a deep sleep when she knocked and that he still has not fully woken up. On her way out, she informs him that the other cassette is from the office of Brian O'Blivion and that she promised she would hand deliver it directly to him.

Max then crosses the room to the television and immediately picks up the videocassette and takes it out of its case. But when he turns it over to examine it, it suddenly pulses and bulges, squirming in his hands as though it were alive and he drops it to the floor. Looking at it again, he realizes that it is clearly an inanimate object and gives it a little tap with his shoe just to make sure. When it doesn't respond, he picks it up and gives it a shake and then slides it into his VCR and presses the play button.

Sitting on the couch across from his television, he watches as Brian O'Blivion abruptly comes onscreen, seated at the very same desk that Max had seen in his study at the Cathode Ray Mission. O'Blivion's monologue begins by informing his audience that the battle for the mind of North America will be fought in the video arena, the Videodrome. He repeats his aphorism from The Rena King Show that the television screen is the retina of the mind's eye, but now he further elaborates that it follows that the television screen is actually part of the physical structure of the brain. Therefore, he says, whatever appears on the television screen emerges as raw experience for those who watch it, and so it follows that television is reality and reality itself is less than television.

When Max chuckles for a moment, O'Blivion addresses him directly by name, telling him that he is glad that Max came to see him. He explains that he has already been through all this himself, and informs Max that his reality is already half video hallucination and that if he is not careful it will become complete hallucination. He tells Max that he will have to learn to live in a very strange new world and as Max watches, puzzled, a hooded figure wearing chainmail steps from behind the tapestry and begins to shackle each of O'Blivion's arms to his chair. The professor, meanwhile, explains that he had a brain tumor and that he also had visions and that he believes that the visions caused the tumor and not the other way around. He says that he could feel the visions coalesce and transform into flesh, but when the tumor was removed, it was called "Videodrome." (Notice the similarity to the image of an embryo being born from the metaphysical vulva that has been interiorized into the male psyche). As the hooded figure then begins to strangle O'Blivion with a garotte, he manages to choke out that he was Videodrome's first victim.

Max, alarmed, gets up from the couch and asks the dying professor who's behind Videodrome and what it is that they want. But when the hooded figure removes the hood, it is revealed to be Nicki Brand, who tells him that she wants *him*.

The camera pulls in tight on her face as she seductively invites him to approach the screen and come to her. Max kneels down in front of the TV as the shot tightens to focus exclusively on Nicki's mouth, with its crescent-bow-shaped lips and white teeth. Max notices the top of his television begin to pulse and throb as though it were alive, while the vinyl lining at its bottom seems to undulate with the sound of Nicki's erotic breathing.

Nicki's mouth in close-up on the screen tells him that she wants him and she wants him now: the glass of the screen transforms into something soft and fleshy as it begins to swell outwards and Max, as though he is about to perform the act of cunnilingus, pushes his face between Nicki's soft lips as her tongue begins to lick his entire head. He palpates the soft flesh-like screen with his hand, and it yields as he puts his head inside of it.

In other words, the Videodrome signal has completely swallowed Max's brain and he now exists *inside* of it, like Jonah in the whale's belly. The image is a macromolecular version of what is taking place inside his brain at the micromolecular scale, as its neurons are being devoured by the electron-corpuscles of the Videodrome signal. Max sticking his head inside of Nicki's mouth is a deterritorialized erotic image—a sort of displacement of coitus from the genitals to the head and mouth which substitute for them—in order to create a kind of assemblage, or indissoluble erotic linkage between Max and the Videodrome signal.

Nicki, in turn, takes Max into her mouth as though he were a kind of communion wafer, for the physical flesh and blood version of Nicki has now disappeared—most likely murdered: the novelization features a scene that was never filmed in which Harlan picks up some Videodrome footage that Max watches of her being tortured[51]—and has been replaced by an electronic avatar. She is the Muse of Videodrome, and the erotic linkage point—just as the receptors on cells are linkage points for drugs—by means of which he will be taken in and connected, cell by cell, to the Videodrome assemblage that will now begin the process of reterritorializing him with a new set of codes.

The image, on another semiotic level, nicely captures with one pictorial glyph McLuhan's idea that television is tactile and that it caresses us with its electron shower. "The TV viewer," he says, "receives these little spots on himself"—referring to electrons—"they wrap around him, he becomes lord of the flies. They settle on him literally. The TV viewer is covered with these little dots, these little flies."[52] The television set palpates the brain and nervous system with its pixilated images, reprogramming the spinal column with its neuronic icons, icons that act as tiny eggs which hatch forth to release new desires that drive the individual toward impulses he or she never knew they had.

It is not a licking of the genitals that television does to us, but rather a licking and sucking of the brain to which it becomes as hopelessly attached as the receptor cells to an opiate addiction.

Archives
(38:56 – 42:35)

In the next shot, an attendant in the Cathode Ray Mission is giving orange juice to a derelict who is sitting in a cubicle watching a game show. She turns away to go about her business just as Bianca O'Blivion informs her that a new group is coming into the Mission in the afternoon and that the attendant needs to inform the staff to be ready for them. Bianca then strides past a long row of cubicles and rounds the corner to the stairwell, where she finds Max Renn seated on the lower steps, waiting for her. He hands back to her the tape cassette and tells her that it was exciting and very lively. As she reaches for it, he then warns her to be careful, as "it bites."

Inside Brian O'Blivion's study, Max crosses the room to glance out the window while Bianca asks him if he watched the cassette. He tells her that he did.

"And?" she says.

"It changed my life," he comments, drily.

She tells him that she's not surprised, for Videodrome is dangerous. Max tries to get her to clarify: because her father admits on the tape that he's somehow involved with Videodrome?

But Bianca explains that there's more to it than that. It bites, as he put it. She then asks him what kind of teeth he thinks it has.

Max says that the tape triggered off a series of hallucinations and that he woke up with a headache.

When she asks whether it was the first time he ever woke up with such a headache, he tells her that he's been hallucinating for a while, and then realizes that he's been hallucinating ever since he first watched Videodrome when Harlan pirated the signal for him off the satellite dish.

Bianca holds up the cassette and informs him that it is part of her own private Videodrome collection. When he says that the tape merely features her father sitting at his desk, she says that the tone of the hallucinations is determined by the tone of the tape's imagery. But the Videodrome signal that does the damage, she explains, can be delivered under anything, even a test pattern.

When Max wants to know what sort of damage she's talking about, she tells him that the signal induces a brain tumor in anyone who watches it and that the tumor is the source of the hallucinations.

Suddenly angry, he stands up and grabs her arm, demanding to know why she let him watch it in the first place.

In defense, she says that she expected "them" to come to her eventually to hurt her and she suspected that it might be him. Now she realizes he's just another victim, like her father.

Max then insists on speaking directly to her father and she tells him that he's "in there," gesturing to a room with double doors, but warns Max that he will probably be disappointed.

When Max opens one of the double doors, he steps into a room full of metal library shelves containing row upon row of videocassettes.

This is all that's left of father, Bianca explains. These are his archives.

When Max asks her what she's talking about, she says that her father died on an operating table eleven months ago. When Max points out that he was on the panel show with him, Bianca says that he was there only on tape, as he made thousands of them, sometimes three or four a day. She says that she keeps him alive as best as she can, while stepping between the aisles to select more tapes for Max to watch.

She explains that her father helped to create Videodrome as the next phase of evolution of man as a technological animal. But then when he realized what his partners were going to use it for, he tried to take it away from them and so they killed him, quietly. At the end of his life, she says, O'Blivion was convinced that public life on television was more real than private life in the flesh and that he wasn't afraid to let his body die.

Max wants her to tell him about his Videodrome problem, but she hands him a stack of tapes, explaining that her father knows much more about it than she does.

Hence, where Max expected to find the real flesh and blood Brian O'Blivion, he finds instead only a semiotic vacancy now occupied by the decorporealized traces left behind by the vanishing of O'Blivion into the matrix. (McLuhan, too, had a brain tumor, but in his case, the operation to remove it was successful and bought him another thirteen years of life, although his writing declined during that period).

One of McLuhan's most famous aphorisms was that when you're on the air, you're no longer in your body.[53]

Hence, one of the side effects of electronic technology is its trading out of cells for electrons, for it is a kind of gigantic cyber-universe in which clones and avatars are replicated like viruses. But these avatars are only two-dimensional images, not the real thing, although they outlive the real flesh and blood individual who generated them by many decades, potentially giving him or her an immortal life span.

That the Videodrome signal creates a brain tumor which transforms one's reality into a living work of contemporary art is another way of saying that life under the conditions of electric saturation replaces the real with the hyperreal, a simulated construct that renders the authentic thing, person or object obsolete. The world, as Jean Baudrillard used to say, is being replaced by its double:[54] electronic technology—and back in the days of the early 1980s such technology was still mostly analogue—is creating an exact duplication of the world, a duplication we have come to prefer over the original. Avatars, Idorus, celebrities, YouTube and Facebook; theme parks, shopping malls and reconstructed archaeological sites; it is all a way of making reality obsolete.

In his 1987 essay on "The Ecstacy of Communication," Baudrillard had described the complete structural alterations that the substitution for the pre-modern assemblage of *scene and mirror* for that of the postmodern assemblage of *screen and network* has created. The change from human scale to nuclear matrices has been effective everywhere, placing an emphasis on the human brain and genes while rendering the entire rest of the physical body, with all its organs, obsolete. The exterior landscape of the real, meanwhile, has been "satellized" by the hyperreal and transformed into a boring desert which no one would wish to cross, while time has shrunk to the instantaneous moment. Public space, too, has been structurally altered by the invasion of advertisements which have had the effect of rendering the "society of the spectacle" obsolete, while private space has been altered by an invasion of one's own home with programming from radio and television that reshape one's private consciousness to the contours of the mediascape. "Thus, the body, landscape, time all progressively disappear as scenes," he concludes.[55] The triumph of the hyperreal over the real has been complete.

Hence, Max Renn's increasing inability to differentiate the real from his hallucinations is really a metonym for *our* inability to distinguish the real from the simulacrum.

And besides: who needs reality, anyway, when the simulacrum is so much more interesting?

Gun / Orifice
(42:36 – 45:56)

The next scene features Max headed purposefully down the hallway of Channel 83 to his secretary's office. He demands to know where Harlan may be found, and Bridey tells him that he's up in V.T.R. Max, frantic, leaves her behind in mid-sentence and then locates Harlan in the tech lab, where he asks him whether he's been hallucinating lately. Harlan tells him that he has not, and asks Max whether he should be? Max replies by saying that yes, he definitely should be, then walks away, leaving a puzzled Harlan behind.

In the next shot, Max is seated on his couch watching the videotaped lectures given to him by Bianca O'Blivion. Professor O'Blivion is explaining that he believes that the growth in his head is not really a tumor but rather an entirely new organ of the brain. He claims that massive doses of the Videodrome signal will create a new outgrowth of the human brain which will produce and control hallucinations to the point that it will change human reality. After all, he says, there is nothing real outside of our perception of reality. Then he laughs briefly and says, "You can see that, can't you?"

Max has been seated on the couch, shirtless, wearing only the shoulder holster of his gun, which he has been clutching in his right hand and using to scratch at a vertical rash that has lately appeared in the center of his torso. After the tape ends, however, he looks down at his torso only to find that the rash has opened up into a pulsing orifice that resembles a lipless vagina. For some bizarre reason unknown even to himself, he uses the gun to probe the slit, then finds himself shoving the gun all the way down inside of it until his hand disappears into his gut. He then stands, hand still buried into the orifice until he yanks it out, but the gun is gone. And when he looks down at his torso, the orifice too has disappeared.

He checks the shoulder holster, but the gun is not there and when he searches the couch, pulling up cushions and pillows, it is nowhere to be found. After a few moments of fruitless searching, the phone rings and he steps over the couch to answer it. A voice on the other end asks if this is Max Renn and when he confirms that it is, the voice tells him that a man named Barry Convex would like to talk to him about Videodrome. The voice further explains that there is a car waiting for Max downstairs.

Now, the wound inflicted into the side of Christ by the spear of the Roman soldier Longinus as Christ was dying on the cross became, in later tradition, recoded as the appropriation of Adam's vaginal cleft—since Christ was the New Adam—from out of which he gave birth to Eve. An image of the wound, appearing vertically just as a vagina would, appears in the 1349 *Prayer and Psalterbook of Bonne de Luxembourg* by Jean Le Noir (shown opposite) where it is thought of as bestowing Christ's infinite grace into the world. But the image, as I have written about elsewhere,[56] is also an appropriation of the metaphysical vulva by the Father who has stolen the procreative powers of the Great Mother during the metaphysical age that extends from Plato to Husserl. This was the age in which the Mother's creative power, still vestigially echoing in Anaximander's *apeiron* (the self-organizing unlimited) became the power of the Word, the Logos of Heraclitus uttered forth as a cosmic structuring principle which, as Heidegger pointed out, with the incarnation of Christ, became restricted to a *single* being.[57]

In *Videodrome*, the vaginal orifice becomes a hallucinatory signifier indicating Max Renn's increasing receptivity to the Videodrome signal. It is actually an image that has been displaced from his brain, which is receiving the signal and softening its neurons to become more malleable to its new codes. Max puts the gun inside the orifice, or rather "inseminates" the orifice since he is unknowingly in the process of being recoded to become an assassin for Spectacular Optical, the corporation which owns Videodrome and wants to use Max to kill Bianca O'Blivion and take over Channel 83 so that they can broadcast the signal on a mass scale.

The image, furthermore, reminds one of something out of a work of contemporary art, by Paul Thek, say, or Anish Kapoor, but that is only because David Cronenberg *is* a contemporary artist who has been displaced to the medium of celluloid. The Videodrome signal transforms one's waking reality into a living work of art, a kind of surrealist virtual reality that slowly comes to stand in for, and replace, physical reality. In other words, it *transubstantiates* physical reality, which is composed of heavy matter—atoms and molecules—into subtle reality, which is self-luminous and composed of photons (which are massless), like an image on a video screen.

That the reality so transformed becomes largely a violent one is testament to the fact that we are living in an image-saturated reality composed largely of Peter Sloterdijk's "disinhibiting media" that have become modern sublimated substitutes for the ancient hippodromes and gladiatorial arenas.[58]

Barry Convex
(45:57 – 54:32)

In the next scene, Max Renn is shown coming down through the lobby of his apartment building wearing his overcoat. He pauses a moment as he looks out through the glass of the front door, then heads down the main walkway to the curb where a silvery-gray stretch limo is waiting for him.[59] He climbs into the backseat, and as the car gets going, the driver tells him to direct his attention to the miniature television screen in front of him, as Barry Convex has already recorded a little introduction for him.

When the screen lights up, a yellow and green eye-shaped logo emerges, then splits in half like an egg to unleash the phrase "Spectacular Optical." Beneath the logo, it says: "Keeping an eye on the world." Then a salesman-looking type of man appears in front of what looks like the red clay wall of the Videodrome set and informs Max that he is Barry Convex, Chief of Special Programs, and that he'd like to invite Max into the world of Spectacular Optical. The miniature televisual image of Convex further informs him that Spectacular Optical makes eyeglasses for the Third World and also missile guidance systems for NATO. He also says that they make Videodrome and that it can be a giant hallucination machine, but also much, much more. It's not ready for the market yet, since what Max picked up were test transmissions that they didn't think anybody would be able to capture.

Max says that Harlan is a good pirate, but at this point Barry does not reveal that Harlan is working for him and not Max.

Convex says that they ought to have a little talk, he and Max, at, say, his place?

The limousine pulls up to the curb in front of a fluorescent-lit sign reading "Spectacular Optical" in green letters above a dingy plate glass window. Max gets out and peers through the dirty glass, then opens the door and browses around trying on various pairs of glasses.

Convex then appears as if from nowhere and warns him that he's playing with dynamite, as those glasses are meant for the spring trade show. He then introduces himself formally and tells Max that the glasses he's wearing are much too large for the shape of his face, and that he should try something more…spidery, more delicate.

In the next shot, however, they are in the back room of the store and Convex is reaching into a large cardboard box from whence he retrieves exactly the opposite of what he'd told Max would look good on him: a huge, bulky, egg-shaped apparatus that resembles an early Virtual Reality machine. (The novelization calls it an "Accumicon," short for "image accumulator.")[60]

He tells Max that the machine is their prototype and that he would like to use it to record one of Max's hallucinations, then take it back to the lab for analysis.

Max makes a joke about keeping the copyright but Convex insists that he's trying to help him. He explains that none of their test subjects have returned to normality and are all in need of intensive psychiatric care, but Max seems to be functioning reasonably well and Convex would like to know why. He thinks an analysis of one of Max's hallucinations would be the right place to start.

Max takes the device and seats himself in a folding chair, asking whether it will hurt. Convex assures him that it will not but that he might catch himself sliding in and out of hallucinatory states afterwards. As he fastens the clip to secure the device to Max's head—which it engulfs entirely (just as Nicki's mouth had done)—Convex explains that a little S&M imagery should be a good way to trigger off a "healthy" series of hallucinations. Something to do, he says, with the effects of exposure to violence on the nervous system, which opens up receptors in the brain and the spine that allow the Videodrome signal to "sink in."

Max asks, jokingly, whether that means he's going to have to hurt Barry—thus foreshadowing the later scene at the trade show when he murders him—but Barry says that won't be necessary since all he need do is just "think about it."

As Convex turns on the machine, Max's visual field is downgraded to a highly pixilated and very low-rez version of the back storeroom. At first the machine is too bright, so Barry shuts off the lights, then flips a switch—presumably the record button—on the back of the helmet, which causes it to light up from within, from whence it gives forth a glowing, pulsing light like the inside of an analogue television.

Max examines his highly pixilated hands for a moment while Barry tells him he doesn't have to do anything now but sit back and hallucinate. Barry says, however, that he will leave Max alone for this, since, as he puts it, he "just can't cope with the freaky stuff."

Max sits in the dark for a few minutes, while the vanilla-colored helmet pulses like a beacon until Nicki Brand appears on the screen in front of him, wearing the red dress he first commented on during the taping of The Rena King Show.

"Nicki?" he says, as her high heels clack across the floor and the pixilation fades completely as Max is engulfed by the entire virtual field of his hallucination.

"Well," she tells him, grabbing a bullwhip from its post on one of the red walls, "Here we are at last…on Videodrome." (Max, of course, is in avataric form, but Nicki no longer has a physical body as source and point of origin; she is composed purely of electrons and photons).

She hands him the bullwhip and he stands up as he recognizes the red room from the taped transmissions of Videodrome.

An old-fashioned console television set has appeared in front of him in place of Nicki, but her face on the screen is in a tight close-up, and her arms are clasped together as though tied to the ceiling as she asks him what he's waiting for: "let's open those neural floodgates, lover," she tells him.

As the camera pulls back, it reveals a pulsing brown television set with Nicki's image on it, the sound of her heavy breathing echoing loudly in the room as Max drags the whip across the walnut veneer top of the set and pulls back closer to the red clay wall to give himself some room. Tentatively at first, he lashes the television with the whip, and when Nicki's voice moans with pleasure, he lashes it again, harder this time.

After several more vigorous lashes, the camera pulls back to reveal that Nicki is no longer on the screen, but that she has been replaced by Masha Borowczyk, wearing Nicki's red dress and moaning with pain, rather than pleasure, in her place.

The novelization of the movie by Jack Martin contains more dialogue about the biography of Barry Convex, who tells Max that he began as a lens grinder, and started with magnifying glasses and microscopes until he worked his way up to designing light weapon scopes for military application (hence the film's otherwise puzzling reference to Spectacular Optical making missile guidance systems for NATO).[61] He says that they designed a kind of fiber optic helmet for soldiers to wear that defied physics by making images visible where images were not supposed to exist—the Accumicon, as it turns out—and that the scopes gave all the soldiers brain cancer. "Came in at the eye," as he comments.[62]

As Convex further elaborates, the soldiers wearing the Accumicons began projecting their own hallucinations into the screen, and so the logic of it was to create a device into which one could simply *think* up his or her own narrative using their own mental imagery. Why spend millions trying to fill the frame with special effects if the Accumicon could be used as a field to receive the images from the contents of one's own mind?[63] "The artists of the future," Convex tells Max, "would be those individuals who could focus their VIDEODROME hallucinations, shape them, control them…"[64]

Convex further explains that they hired Nicki Brand because they needed a professional, psychological interpretation of the hallucinatory graphics.[65] So there is some ambiguity about whether Nicki Brand was murdered or whether she is still alive and working for Spectacular Optical.

Either way, it becomes clear from this sequence that David Cronenberg—like media theoreticians such as Neil Postman, William Irwin Thompson,[66] Morris Berman[67] and others—is skeptical of such image-generating technologies, and is especially mistrustful of the mediatized images of sex and violence that they spray at the crowds the way trucks in the 1950s used to go merrily along through suburban neighborhoods spraying the streets with "harmless" DDT. The capturing of Max Renn's head by the device that "records" his hallucinations—hallucinations, that is, that have already been caused by his exposure to the Videodrome signal—is actually a perfect metaphor for what has happened to all of us in the society in which the real has been replaced by the precession of Baudrillard's simulacra: there is a Videodrome helmet that has captured each and every one of our heads inside of it and is spray-painting our visual cortex, through our eyes, with appalling images of violence that do indeed open up neural floodgates by activating the emotionless reptilian brain stem, with its fight or flight instincts. By distracting the rationality of the brain's frontal lobe with glittering images of consumer products, it meanwhile sends disinhibiting images past the frontal lobe when it's not looking, and those amongst us who are susceptible to violence turn to it because the mediatized images have told them that violence is the normal response. As the Geico ads go: it's what everyone does.

Our children are especially susceptible to these images—think of Sandyhook—and because the only anthropomorphic types they have to draw from in order to model their lives after are celebrities—weak, narcissistic and ego-centric models—the images act in place of true anthropomorphic types and become what Cornelius Castoriadis called "imaginary significations" all their own.[68] That is why so many spree killers are young and tend to range from the ages of about 15 to 25. Their brains are still labile, still developing and still highly suggestible and they have emerged out of a social environment of decaying institutions like public schools and psychiatric clinics which help them to form little in the way of a psychological immune system to keep the images at bay.

The irony of Cronenberg's work is that as a lapsed Jew he comes out of an iconophobic tradition, yet his films are packed with images of sex and violence. He is using an iconophilic culture, however—with all its media apparatus: film, celluloid, special effects and cameras—to cast a skeptical eye upon the dangerous, anti-social effects of the propagation of its images. His later 1999 film *Existenz* is even more skeptical of this "society of the icon," focusing on the rise of ever more and more "realistic" video game images which routinely feature violence as entertainment.

During the height of the Byzantine Civilization, the Iconoclastic Controversy that occurred between the years 727 - 843 AD was a direct result of the influence upon that civilization of the iconophobic society of Islam (particularly Arabic, or "Western" Islam), with which it was perpetually at war. The iconoclasts argued that it was blasphemy—according to the Old Testament, at least—to attempt to represent the Divine in the form of images (in addition to having the taint of idolatry about it), but John of Damascus (675 – 749) and Theodore the Studite (759 – 826) argued that the whole point of the Incarnation was to make the invisible spiritual reality of the Divine visible by pouring God forth into human form, thus annulling the Old Testament ban on the representation of images. The image, furthermore, was not identical in substance with the Divine, but only "resembled" it. The iconoclasts, needless to say, lost the debate and the widow of emperor Theophilus restored the cult of images in 843.[69] Hence, those visions of saints and Christ Pantocrator and the Virgin Mary passed over into the iconophilic West via places like Ravenna and

Florence, which received these iconotypes as the sinking ship of Constantinople was gradually submerged and recoded by the Ottomans, who finally took the city in 1453 (just about the time that the West was inventing the printing press). The West has been an "iconophilic" culture ever since.

But now Islamic fundamentalist culture—traditionally iconophobic—under the influence of the iconophilic West (especially in its electronic phase) is using Western iconophilic technologies—video, television, YouTube—in order to make its points, and so the influence is now running the other way—from West to East—and Islam is in danger, without knowing it, of becoming just as iconophilic as the West. They have discovered the power of images like beheadings and bombings to "open up those neural floodgates" to make the brain receptive to their message, in their case, that of a Boundary Act that is designed to use the mediatized images as a kind of decorporealized wall to keep the West *out*.[70]

Thus, the planet is currently locked in a war of images and icons transmitted via media apparatuses of all kinds, for images are now actually being used by both civilizations as weapons. So, as David Cronenberg correctly foresaw in 1983, such images can indeed become dangerous.

Corpse / Corpuscle
(54:33 – 58:34)

In the next scene, Max is shown waking up from a nightmare in the pinkish-blue light of his bedroom. The television set across the hall is tuned to a snowy channel. He mutters a question to himself: what's going on, Professor O'Blivion? Then he lies back, puts a pillow on his head and rolls over on his right side where he unexpectedly encounters a solid figure under the sheets. He pulls the sheet back to reveal a dead woman in his bed, her wrists tied together with a leather strap, and when he rolls her toward him he sees that it is Masha, her mouth bound with a gag, eyes open and fishbelly white.

He jumps out of bed, frightened, then covers up Masha's body with a sheet.

He goes into the living room and picks up the telephone, then punches the buttons of Harlan's number and when Harlan answers, he tells him to come over to his apartment right away and that he has a very serious situation on his hands.

In the next shot, a groggy Harlan is entering Max's apartment, camera with flashbulb dangling from his neck as he asks Max what's going on.

Max tells him he wants Harlan to go into his bedroom and take a look at what's in his bed and that he wants pictures of it, but Harlan is skeptical. Nevertheless, he agrees and opens the glass doors leading to Max's bedroom where he stands a moment, expressionless, before coming back out and telling Max that he didn't see anything.

Max, in consternation, runs into his bedroom and begins to search for the missing corpse of Masha, just as he had done earlier with the gun that had disappeared into his abdomen.

Harlan asks him whether he's in some kind of drug warp and that he knows friends who can help, but Max cuts him off and asks him if he taped Videodrome last night. Harlan says that yes, if it was transmitted, the machine would've caught it. Max then tells him to meet him in the lab in one hour, but when Harlan protests that it's not even 7 a.m. Max loses his temper and yells that he is not just fucking around. Harlan tells him to go fuck himself and that he is not just some servomechanism that Max can shut on and off at will. If Max wants him to fall out of bed and run around for him like an asshole then he needs to know what he's doing it for.

Max calms down and apologizes, telling him that momentum is carrying him forward like an express train and that he can't stop. He tells Harlan he'll meet him in the lab in an hour and when they look at the Videodrome transmission from the previous night, he'll explain everything.

Mollified, Harlan apologizes at the front door for freaking out and Max offers to make him a cup of coffee but then quickly changes his mind and tells him he'll meet him in the lab in an hour.

Now, the interesting thing about this brief scene is that it is the first time in the narrative that a decorporealized human being has appeared within the frame of Max's physical reality. Thus far, only physical objects like televisions, tape cassettes or possibly the gun—other than the slap he imagined giving to Bridey—have appeared within the field of Max's physical material reality. Whenever he had encountered Nicki after she left for Pittsburgh, it was always within the context of a mediated visual field, either on Videodrome or within the virtual reality of the Accumicon.

But with Masha's corpse appearing in his bed, he is now beginning to realize that his brain can project images of physical human beings within his waking reality, decorporealized phantoms whose corpuscles have been traded out for electrons and photons, like the decorporealized avatars projected by the cathode ray tube on a television screen. Reality, in other words, has become a screen for Max upon which absolutely anything or anyone can appear. He has become a walking cathode ray tube and what Professor O'Blivion warned would happen to him is now happening: his reality is slowly telemorphosizing into a complete video hallucination. It is no longer possible for either Max—or for that matter, the viewer of the film—to differentiate whether the people Max is seeing are real or Videodrome avatars.

We do not know whether Masha is alive or not, but in the novelization there follows an interesting scene in which Max draws a bath for himself and to his amazement, a television console crawls up from out of the bathwater with an image of Masha on its screen.[71] She informs him that she was murdered for giving him the name of Brian O'Blivion and tells him that he has now become the video word made flesh. The film, however, leaves it uncertain whether Masha is still alive or not—though we never see her again—just as there is some ambiguity about whether Nicki Brand is still alive (though she most likely is not). But Nicki Brand, as the muse of Videodrome, never appears in unmediated form: she is the mistress of the matrix and always interfaces with Max via television screen, Accumicon or tape cassette, and this mediation suggests that she has become an electron ghost, her physical body dead—like the construct of the Dixie Flatline in *Neuromancer*—while her plasmic phantom has been resurrected into the Electron Afterlife of the video matrix.

Max's world is now slowly becoming populated by ghosts and phantoms as the Real keeps steadily slipping further and further away from him. (Vilem Flusser has termed this phenomenon of the slippage of technological images from their material substrates "Immaterialism.")[72]

Programming Max
(58:35 – 1:03:57)

There follows an exterior shot of Max entering the Civic TV building early in the morning before anyone else has gotten there. He is then shown going down the staircase leading to the sub-basement—as though descending into the Underworld—where he knocks on the door to the lab and Harlan lets him in.

Max asks Harlan if he's looked at the tape and seen him on Videodrome, but Harlan candidly tells him there *was* no tape. Max, surprised, asks him to clarify: there *was* no Videodrome transmission the previous night? Harlan replies no, not last night, not ever. Max, confused, then asks him what he's talking about while there comes a knock at the door. Harlan says he's out of his depth now and has to bring in the reinforcements.

He opens the door as a smugly smiling Barry Convex enters, dressed in a three-piece suit, and greets him. "An intriguing combination," Max says, "Very interesting."

Convex insists that they not let him interrupt and Max says he was saying something like 'What are you talking about?'

Harlan explains that he was playing pre-recorded tapes of Videodrome for Max to watch and that Videodrome has never been transmitted on an open broadcast circuit.

Max says that Barry sent him to work for him about, what, two years ago?

To which Harlan replies without any trace of irony: "Two wonderful years."

When Max asks him why, Harlan tells him that it was to get him involved by exposing him to the Videodrome signal.

Max now realizes that the signal never affected Harlan because he never actually watched the tapes, as he already knew what was on them.

Harlan points out that the signal really does work on just about anybody, and at this point Barry elaborates, "anybody who watches it," and then poses the question of why anybody *would* watch such a scum show in the first place. When he asks Max why *he* watched it, Max replies, pragmatically, "for business reasons." Barry asks him, though, about the *other* reasons: why doesn't Max admit that he gets his kicks out of watching images of torture and murder?

Max counters by accusing him of murdering Brian O'Blivion and asks him whether he enjoyed *that*.

Harlan then goes into a speech about how North America is getting soft while the rest of the world is getting tough. He explains that we're now entering savage new times and that we're going to have to be pure and direct and strong in order to survive them. He claims that this cesspool of a TV station Max calls Channel 83 is rotting "us" away from the inside and that they, he and Barry Convex, intend to stop that rot.

Barry steps in and tells Max that they intend to use Channel 83 to start their first authentic transmissions of Videodrome and that he has a hunch it will be *very* popular.

Max says he must be hallucinating right now because he doesn't believe Barry and Harlan can possibly be for real.

Then as he is about to leave the lab, Barry stops him and says that they *did* record and analyze his hallucinations on the Accumicon and that he thinks Max is now ready for something new.

Max tells him, sarcastically, "That's terrific," but Barry pulls a videocassette from out of his jacket, one that is pulsing and squirming once again.

A strange wind from nowhere begins to blow against Max, and he asks, backing away against the door, what Barry wants from him. Barry calmly explains that he just wants Max to "open up" for him (Max, in return, will later "open up" Barry by different means). Max's shirt then splits apart as though invisible hands were pulling on it, buttons popping off, to reveal the vaginal orifice in his lower abdomen that is also pulsating and dilating, as though eager to receive the cassette.

Barry steps forward and tells Max that he's got something he wants to play for him and then thrusts the tape cassette into the orifice while Max screams. Barry yanks his hand out and the tape cassette is gone. Max slumps to the floor and coughs, while Barry and Harlan, without further word, exit from the room.

Of course, there is here the obvious analogy of Max as a human VCR who will play the tape of becoming an assassin for Spectacular Optical.[73] That is the symbolic content of his hallucination, which rhymes with the earlier scene in which he had shoved the phallic gun into the same vaginal orifice. Whereas that scene had connotations of a sexual coitus that will produce the gun-as-embryo of the scene that will follow next, the present scene has more to do with inserting codes into Max that will "program" him to perform acts of violence that he otherwise would never have done.

Hence, he has gone from being the president of a cable television station looking for fresh content to program it with, to himself becoming programmed by the very show that he had thought he had discovered that would put his station on the media map with a breakthrough. Thus, he is not only a human VCR, but he has become the content of Videodrome itself and his life is about to open out into its red room without walls, for he himself will soon begin to spread throughout the city all the violence and mayhem that thus far he has only seen on Videodrome or else projected as hallucination.

The video word is, indeed, now about to become flesh.

Gun Embryo
(1:03:58 – 1:06:08)

In this scene, Max drags himself along the floor out of the lab as he hears the voice of Barry Convex in his head telling him that they want Channel 83 and that they want him to kill his two partners. He crawls into a corner and pulls himself into a seated position against a wall with cracked plaster that looks like something out of an Alberto Burri *White Cretto* composition.

As he breathes painfully—like a woman in labor—he reaches his right hand into the glistening slit in his torso in an attempt to remove the cassette, but instead what it retrieves is the gun that he had inserted into it several days ago. The black metallic carapace of the Walther PPK is covered in mucus and dripping a gelatinous substance as he holds it out before him, while strange metallic tentacles begin to emerge from his lower three fingers and dig into the palm of his hand. Two more tentacles emerge from the gun itself, and all five of them begin burrowing into his wrist bone, snaking up his arm and fusing with its cartilage and marrow.

The gun has now become permanently fused with his body, and he hears the voice of Barry Convex in his head once more instructing him to kill his partners (Moses and Raphael) and give Channel 83 over to Spectacular Optical.

Now, one of McLuhan's most important aphorisms is that technology constitutes various extensions of the human anatomy. The wheel, for instance, is an extension of the foot; clothing is an extension of the skin; a house is an extension of the immune system; and electronic circuitry is an extension of the nervous system.[74] (Note that this latter point means that the entire earth has been surrounded and encased inside of the human nervous system through the process of its satellization, as Baudrillard terms it).

A gun is simply a mechanized updating of such ancient ballistic weapons as spears, arrows and slingshots. Those weapons, in turn—as ancient as the vast depths of the remote mists of the Paleolithic dawn—were extensions of the teeth, fangs and claws which the anthropoid human gradually gave up in exchange for an ever larger and larger frontal lobe that was able to exteriorize them in order to compete with dangerous animals.

Guns, then, are extensions of human aggression that simply render spears and arrows—which in turn had obsolesced the fangs and claws of wolves, lions and leopards—obsolete.

But the other half of McLuhan's point—and since *Videodrome* is a film that specifically explores McLuhan's ideas, it is appropriate to invoke him continually throughout this exegesis—is that the part of the anatomy so extended by technology becomes numbed by the extension.[75] If the wheel extends the foot into what Paul Virilio calls the "dromosphere,"[76] it can no longer feel the earth and the body's proper orientation to it is numbed as it is sent speeding by means of one or another vehicle that sends it crashing into some other vehicle whose occupant has also traded out his feet for wheels.

Max, as I have said, is now completely engulfed by the Videodrome signal and his reality has become constant and continuous hallucination, just as Professor O'Blivion warned him it would. In his present hallucination, his body has simply incorporated the gun inside of it just the way it would incorporate any technological object such as a pacemaker or a metallic hip replacement. The metaphoric content of the hallucination, though, means that the gun has actually fused together with his psyche and become inseparable from it, for he has degenerated from the president of a cable television network to a disheveled spree killer whose brain can no longer separate the fusion of his neurons from the Videodrome electrons. The gun has fused with his arm, just as reality has fused together with his hallucinations. The simulacrum, exactly as in Baudrillard's 1981 essay on "The Precession of Simulacra," now *precedes* and displaces the real. Max no longer has any way of distinguishing between the Real and the Imaginary orders, for the Lacanian L-schema designed specifically to separate them, and keep them separate, has collapsed.

His capture by the Videodrome signal is complete.

Spree Killer
(1:06:09 – 1:08:42)

Now Max is shown calmly walking up the staircase of Channel 83, expressionless as coworkers pass him by and say hello while he ignores them. He goes straight to Bridey's office and asks her where his partner Moses can be found, and she says that he's in a meeting with Raphe. She picks up the phone and offers to notify them that he's coming in, but he firmly places the phone back into its cradle and tells her, "Don't." He walks slowly toward the closed doors of the conference room, looks both ways, then enters it and shuts the door behind him, quietly.

Moses and Raphael are having a conversation about how they could improve a video series by turning it into a comedy—perhaps *Samurai Dreams*, as the novelization suggests[77]—and when they see him, Moses says that Max is just in time to shed some light on an interesting problem.

But Max calmly pulls the gun out of his jacket, cocks the barrel and points it at Raphael, who raises his arms to defend himself while a bullet rips into his elbow, followed by two more that puncture his torso, killing him.

Moses, meanwhile, is climbing slowly up from his chair and as Max approaches him with the gun, he falls back against the wall, muttering, "Max, what the fuck?" He then slides down the wall as Max fires two bullets into his head at point blank range. Blood spurts like a geyser from the back of his skull, spraying onto the wall behind him.

The door opens and Bridey rushes in, while Max hides the gun under his jacket, pretending to be shot. When Bridey asks him if he is ok, he tells her that "they killed us," as he stumbles out of the room, screams erupting all around him. Bridey guides him past the soda machine and asks to see his wound, but Max gets up and heads for the delivery entrance. Bridey, puzzled, asks after him, but he doesn't know what to say and gives her a somber look as he shoves the door open to exit into the alleyway where movers are unloading doors into the studio. He hurries past them, pulls out the gun, zips up his jacket and then puts the gun in his right jacket pocket.

Then he heads off for the Cathode Ray Mission.

The spree killer constitutes a sort of social auto-immune disorder, but not one that happens merely by chance. Both John Hinckley, jr. and Mark David Chapman, for instance, were inspired to their murderous deeds—although Chapman was successful in killing John Lennon, while Ronald Reagan barely escaped Hinckley's bullet alive—specifically by media images, as I have remarked in the Introduction. Hinckley was so captivated by the image avatar of Jodi Foster in *Taxi Driver* that it deranged him into attempting to murder Ronald Reagan in order to impress her, while Mark David Chapman could not tolerate the ambiguities of Lennon's various media personae and thought he was a "phony" and a hypocrite. Valerie Solanas, likewise, shot Andy Warhol because she claimed that he had "captured" her mind and wouldn't let it go. And Andrew Cunanan shot and killed Gianni Versace because he was so captivated by Versace's media persona that he knew the act would make him famous.[78]

The Videodrome signal is metaphoric of the power of mediatized images to enter into the psyche and destabilize it with all the force of psycho-pharmaceuticals that disrupt one's moods by shifting chemicals around in the brain. Such chemicals cannot be jumbled about without producing serious side effects, and the side effects of a culture that has become hyper-saturated by "disinhibiting" media images is the production of unstable personalities. While I don't think there is a direct cause and effect relationship between the viral proliferation of these images and deranged individuals, the over-saturation of such psyches developing within a society in which image swarms have pushed everything else out can, I think, be said to "encourage" such deranged individuals to enact the more violent images upon the social scene. Humans are mimetic animals and from early childhood on they like to imitate what they see going on around them.

Thus, in a hunting society that is based upon the killing and eating of animals as the primary nourishment and way of life, the rituals and narratives tend to involve people wearing animal skins and pretending to *be* animals. In early Neolithic agrarian societies, where plants form the center and focus of life, human sacrifice is enacted to illustrate the myth of the origins of the main food plant, for the willing victim always incarnates and "plays" the role of the proto-plant (i.e. maize, calabash, wheat, etc.)[79]

So we should not be the least bit surprised that in a culture that is surrounded by movies and television shows featuring people solving their problems with violence, that we have produced a culture that is packed with spree killers who imitate the images they see beaming at them at light speed from the various media apparatuses surrounding them everywhere they look.

Thus, the Videodrome signal has entered into Max's body like the power of the Logos through a communion wafer that gathers the individual up into the mystical body of Christ. Max Renn is now translating the images of Videodrome into actuality as the video word made flesh. His actions are becoming imitations of Videodrome performances in the arena of physical matter. Images made out of light and electrons have entered into him through the eye and have spread through the cells of his body like a cancer.

The Video Word Made Flesh
(1:08:43 – 1:13:27)

It is now nighttime and Max is shown coming up the sidewalk in front of the Cathode Ray Mission. Barry Convex's voice inside his head tells him to kill Bianca O'Blivion because she knows too much and she can hurt them. But when Max tries the front door, it is locked, and a sign reads "CLOSED FOR ALTERATIONS."

He goes around to the back of the building, pushing open the gate to a chain link fence while the sound of a jet plane passes overhead. The back doors of the Mission have Gothic-shaped glass windows which he simply smashes in with his elbow and then reaches down to unlock the door, stepping into a darkened hallway. He walks past a room with a few scattered cubicles and then notices a rectangle of vanilla-colored light coming from another smaller room just past it where a desk with the remains of a recently eaten meal and a typewriter are splayed across it. He hears a door open and close somewhere and then approaching footsteps, so he carefully steps back into the shadows as Bianca O'Blivion, carrying a stack of videocassettes, comes around the corner.

As she enters the room with the cubicles where Max is standing, he says her name and she turns around. He explains that he runs Civic TV, as though they had never met (he is losing his autonomy as the signal hollows him out), and tells her that he was on a talk show with her father.

"So it was to be you after all," she says, realizing that he's come to kill her.

But he says, zombie-like, that he is Max Renn and that he runs Civic TV and that he doesn't kill people. (Hence, McLuhan's point that violence is a quest for identity, and once private identity is scrapped by rapid technological innovation, people tend to resort to violence, as in David Cronenberg's 2012 film *Cosmopolis*, in which a man who loses his fortunes betting on the stock market resorts to murder as his identity is scrapped in a matter of hours).[80]

Bianca insists, however, that he *does* kill people and that he has become an assassin now for Videodrome. She tells him that they can program him like a videotape recorder and that they can make him do anything they want. And what they want him to do now is to destroy whatever is left of Brian O'Blivion. She tells him, backing away into the shadows, that they want Max to destroy her.

He unzips his jacket as she retreats and when his hand comes out, it is no longer a human hand at all, but rather a strange new organ that has become a complete fusion of metal and biology, no longer recognizable as a hand holding a gun at all, but as a hand-gun organic assemblage. Bone and cartilage have grown over the metal, completely incorporating it into Max's body the way a tree might continue growing around a metal fence pole by simply taking it up into its anatomy.

She dodges him on the other side of the cubicles, weaving in and out between them as he attempts to keep track of her, but she disappears behind a partition and the sound can be heard of her loading her own weapon: the distinct clicking of a tape being pushed into a VCR.

When he approaches the cubicle, which is irradiating a coffee-colored light through the brown paper, he tears through the paper with his hand to reveal a television set that is playing the tape of Nicki Brand's murder on Videodrome. He watches while a gloved hand chokes her to death and Bianca informs him, from somewhere in the shadowy corners of the room, that they killed Nicki. Bianca says that Nicki died on Videodrome and that they used her image to seduce him but she was already dead.

As he begins to step backwards, Bianca tells him not to back away: she stole the tape from them specifically for him to see it. The tape then stops and Bianca's voice tells him that Videodrome is death. When he looks back at the television it has become a snowy image, but a living one as an arm with a gun at the end of it pushes through the snowy image as though the screen were made of something as malleable as plastic, covered with dots like flies. But as he watches, the flies disappear, and the armed gun hand is seen to be pushing through an elongating epidermal membrane.

He raises his own gun-hand assemblage as though to fire at it, but the flesh gun from the television console turns slightly in response and then shoots precisely three bullets into Max's torso. He falls to his knees, and the image on the TV console then changes to that of a bare human torso with three bleeding bullet wounds in it, mirroring his own. (It is Cronenberg's postmodern recoding of the Archaic Torso of Apollo, only now the torso is embedded in the television console because Max Renn has been captured and exists completely within a telemorphosized reality).

But Max's death is only symbolic, for as he falls to the floor, supporting himself with one hand, Bianca tells him, "That's much better," for it is always painful to remove the cassette. It is a ritual recoding that she is putting him through as she steps forward holding a cassette in her hand to stand between him and the snowy image on the television screen that has reverted back to its normal mode behind her.

She tells him that now he has become something quite different than he was before: he has become, as Masha in the novelization first informed him, the video word made flesh.

He repeats the phrase ritualistically: I am the video word made flesh.

She says that now that he *is* the video word made flesh, he knows what he must do. He must turn against Videodrome and use the weapons they've given him to destroy *them*.

Death to Videodrome.

Long live the new flesh.

Max repeats this catechism as he is recoded now to become an assassin for the Cathode Ray Mission.

Nicki Brand and Bianca O'Blivion form a counter pole: for whereas Nicki was tortured and murdered like one of the female Christian saints—St. Eulalia, say, who was tortured by the Romans and left to die, while a sifting of snow covered her dead body, just as the snowy television screen followed and, as it were, covered up the video-taped image of Nicki's death—Bianca O'Blivion is more like Athena, the virgin patroness of soldiers and goddess of wisdom and the arts. Bianca organizes the files of her father's mind, just as Athena was born from the mind of her father Zeus, and she has one thing that Spectacular Optical—which, as the name implies, specializes in the Eye—does not possess: the power of the vulva and the Great Mother's command over the physical body. She puts Max Renn—whose last name, as remarked, suggests rebirth—through a death and resurrection process and shows him his body on the television console, which has become reterritorialized as the womb through which he is being reborn. (Whereas, once Nicki had been killed and reborn as the Muse of Videodrome, the focus was on her eyes and especially her mouth, which devoured Max's head).

Nicki, then, is associated with eyes and mouth; Bianca—whose name resembles her father's, Brian—is associated with the metaphysical vulva and the actual physical body itself. She retains the power of the ancient Great Mother to confer rebirth on all who kneel before her, just as in the ancient world, the initiates of the cult of Isis—the prototype of the icon which later became the Virgin in Coptic Egypt[81]—bowed before her transformative powers.

She has used her own access to Videodrome—since she has remained at its point of origin in her father's Cathode Ray Mission—to send three bullets into Max: one for body, one for soul, and one for spirit or mind. Like a soldier under the protection of Athena, he is now a soldier of the Cathode Ray Mission and an initiate in the cult of its goddess, and he has been recoded to become its primary warrior.

His task now is to send a spear through the All Seeing Eye of Spectacular Optical.

Killing Harlan
(1:13:28 – 1:18:02)

The next morning, Max is shown standing across the street from Spectacular Optical, carefully watching to see who comes and goes. A homeless man with a small black and white television set stands nearby, and Max listens as the newscaster reports that a bizarre and apparently motiveless shooting took place at Civic TV, a shooting which has triggered off an intensive manhunt for its president, Max Renn. The derelict holds his silver begging dish up to Max and tells him that if he wants to see the monkey dance, he needs to pay the piper. As Max's Walther PPK is shown on the small black and white screen, the derelict explains to Max that the cold kills his monkey's batteries.

Meanwhile, Max spots Harlan, wearing his usual plaid shirt and vest, entering through the front door of Spectacular Optical and so he crosses the street to follow him in. When he steps inside the front lobby, a woman is trying on a pair of glasses while other customers are waiting, one of them a policeman, whom Max is careful to dodge. A salesman comes out from behind the counter and tells Max that his name is Brolley and asks how he can help him. Max tells him that he's just looking and the salesman laughs and says there isn't much to see here but he's welcome to have a look anyway, then moves on to help another customer with her 'scrip.

Max takes advantage of the diversion to sneak his way past the counter into the back room, where he finds Harlan at work taping up a large cardboard box. Max smiles, walks past him, looks into the other back room where some people are busy working, then turns on his heels and asks Harlan where Convex is to be found.

Harlan explains that Convex is busy setting up his trade show for the spring line.

Max walks past the box, pats it, and asks what's in it.

Harlan tells him that he has Max's head in the box (meaning, I take it, the Accumicon that Convex used to record his hallucinations).

Harlan then tells Max that he's been reading about him in the papers. He asks him whether he's been to see Bianca O'Blivion, to which Max replies that he did indeed see her. Harlan asks whether she gave him any trouble and Max responds with a casual, "No."

Harlan suggests that maybe Max would like to visit somebody else now and asks him if that is why he has come there? "Maybe," Max replies, smiling secretively.

Harlan tells him that Max has been very useful to them and that they'd like to keep on using him up until he's all gone. Then Harlan produces another videocassette to program Max with, but this one is not only breathing and pulsing, it is also diseased and sickly-looking. (It is possible that they intend to use it to infect Max with a disease that will kill him).

Harlan demands that he open up to him, and Max steps confidently forward and unbuttons his shirt. Harlan, echoing Barry Convex, says that he has something he wants to play for Max and shoves the cassette into Max's vaginal orifice. This time, however, Max bears down hard on it and Harlan begins to struggle to pull his hand out as a mysterious wind blows against him.

When Harlan, terrified, finally yanks his hand out of the orifice, it has been sheared into a bloody stump and somehow transformed into a ticking bomb.

Max calmly buttons up his shirt as a frightened Harlan backs away from him, while coworkers, seeing the bloody stump, begin screaming.

Max tells Harlan he will see him in Pittsburgh, and as Harlan is backed against a wall, the bomb-hand explodes, blowing a hole through the wall and scattering pieces of Harlan's body everywhere.

Max, smiling grimly, steps through the hole and out into the back alley, on his way to the Spectacular Optical trade show.

Thus, Bianca O'Blivion's recoding of Max has not only consisted of a baptism by blood, but she has also morphologically altered the bio-weapons given to him by the Videodrome executives. The vaginal orifice has been transformed from being merely a passive receiver of programmed tapes, to becoming a *vagina dentata* (indeed teeth can be glimpsed in a careful freeze frame of the shot with Harlan's hand inside the orifice just after he pulls it out) capable, not only of ripping a man's hand clean off the bone, but also of transforming it into a time bomb.

It is possible that Max somehow remade the diseased videocassette itself into a bomb using the newly acquired warrior powers given to him by the Athena-like Bianca O'Blivion. (The name "Bianca," incidentally, is an Italian cognate of French *Blanche*, meaning "white." Hence, she

117

is Robert Graves's White Goddess of the moon, with its three phases [new, full and crescent]—in disguise.[82] This is perhaps also why she shoots him with precisely three bullets).

The explosive power of the metaphysical vulva and all its transformations which are associated with the Great Goddess has now been demonstrated to Videodrome and its conspirators.

Spring Trade Show
(1:18:03 – 1:21:18)

Max now pulls open the lobby doors of a hotel that is featuring Spectacular Optical's Spring Trade Show. He goes over to the reception desk and grabs a brochure, pretending to be a patron as he walks past a sign that reads: "SPECTACTULAR OPTICAL WELCOMES YOU: DISPLAYS OF OUR NEW LINE MEDICI."

Inside the large conference room, there has been set up a stage adorned with kitschy signifiers from the Renaissance: men and women dressed in Renaissance clothing cavort about the stage as though enacting scenes from the paintings of Andrea Mantegna or Masaccio. A giant, gaudy pair of eyeglasses sits in front of a poor imitation of Michelangelo's God Awakening Adam from the Sistine Ceiling. (Note that the spark given to the inert mass of Adam by God now becomes, in *Videodrome*, the electronic signal that destroys one's brain, bringing not a body to life, but a swarm of phantasms). An oval-shaped sign has been placed at either end of the stage, one with the quote "The eye is the window to the soul" and the other reading "Love comes in at the eye."

As Max makes his way about between the crowded tables, a man dressed in Renaissance garb onstage pretends to be Michelangelo chiseling away at a marble block, causing its two halves to fall away to reveal a portrait bust of some sort.

Max finds an empty seat at a table and sits down, pretending to read his brochure as a musical number unfolds onstage, in which three female dancers—like the classical Three Graces—shed their outfits to reveal sexier, Busby Berkeley-type outfits beneath. They begin to dance to more contemporary showtunes music, holding fake eyeglasses on sticks up to their faces.

Max notices a woman walking around with a concession box hanging from her neck, only instead of food or cigars, she is selling eyeglasses. The box is labeled "Medici."

The musical number ends and then Barry Convex, microphone in hand, steps out onto the stage and tells the audience that they all know him and he certainly all knows them, every single one of them. Max, with his back turned to the stage, realizes who is speaking and slowly turns round as the audience applauds. He sits a moment to listen to Convex's speech, which goes on about celebrating the arrival of their spring collection. He tells the audience that the theme for this year is based on two quotes from Lorenzo de Medici: "Love comes in at the eye," and "The eye is the window to the soul."

Now the former quote is certainly older than Lorenzo de Medici, for it was an idea of the troubadours that love blossomed with a meeting of the eyes.[83] And it was at about the time of the troubadours that the first eyeglasses in the West were being made in Italy.

The idea that the eye is the window to the soul contains an entire optical theory inside of it, since for the Greeks the eye was a solid thing—especially articulated in Euclid's *Optica*—that was thought to function either by receiving atoms that bombarded it from the outer world or else, more bizarrely, actually shed emanations from it. The eye was not even considered to be hollow until about 200 – 300 AD when, in late Roman portrait statues, such as those of Decius or the philosopher Dogmatius, the Roman artists began drilling holes into the pupils. But it was not until the Arabian philosopher Alhazen wrote his *Book of Optics* around the year 1000, which the West inherited when it was translated into Latin by the end of the twelfth century, that the eye was imagined to be hollow and to actually *receive* light rays through the pupil that was like a miniature oculus.[84] It cannot be a coincidence that once the correct theory of the way in which the eye receives light through a lens was worked out that the first eyeglasses were then invented in Italy around 1286.

The Videodrome signal, too, enters in through the eye—just as in the novelization Barry Convex points out that his Accumicon caused soldiers to get brain cancer which "came in at the eyes"—and creates the tumor as a new organ of the brain that then *transmits*, rather than merely *receives* images in the form of hallucinations. Cronenberg, with his Vegas-style stage set, is actually performing an image archaeology on the idea of his tumor-causing Videodrome signal that turns the brain into a biological cathode ray tube.

As Convex continues with his sales pitch, Max rises from the table, clearly revealing his biomechanical gun-hand assemblage as he steps up onto the stage and confronts Barry Convex. When Convex recognizes him, he attempts to flee, but Max follows him across the stage and fires three bullets into his torso and one into his head. Convex collapses and Max watches as the bullets—which are no ordinary bullets but cancerous tumors that erupt and burst apart the insides of Convex's body—split his head open, causing his internal organs to rupture and squirm. The assassination is Max's response to Barry's earlier insistence that he "open up for him."

Max picks up the microphone and shouts into it: "Death to Videodrome! Long live the new flesh!"

Then he throws the microphone down and while Convex's body continues to rupture and split apart right down the center, Max hurries through the lobby and out the front door before anyone has time to recognize him.

Bianca O'Blivion has indeed given Max some new weapons: not only has she given him teeth in the vaginal orifice opened up in him by the Videodrome signal, but her powers have caused the bullets of his gun to be remade as cancerous tumors capable of multiplying with incredible speed that rip Barry Convex apart from within, since Max himself is now captured on the inside of Videodrome. It is therefore precisely *inside* Videodrome that he can himself function like a tumor to destroy it from within and since, in a certain sense, Barry Convex stands metonymically as part for the whole of Videodrome, it is appropriate that he is ruptured internally, as though Max were inside his body attacking it at a micromolecular level. Max has become the cancer that has invaded the mystical body of Videodrome.

One more note on this particular scene: the Renaissance theme is not an accident because for Marshall McLuhan the fifteenth and sixteenth centuries constituted a crucial epoch in Western civilization, for it was the time when the eye, with the new optical theories discussed above, began to perceive space in realistic, three-dimensional terms.[85] The fifteenth century is the time when the Italians, from Masaccio and Donatello onwards, created depth perspective using Euclidean geometry, and visualized space as a container inside which all objects were situated and subordinated to a single point of view. All objects were thus thought to be part of the same shared space, whereas in the Medieval epoch, each object occupied its own space and could therefore be represented as any size whatsoever in relation to any other objects, just as Christ and the Virgin Mary are often represented as larger and out of scale with the rest of the figures[86] (Grunewald's Crucifixion at the center of the Isenheim Altarpiece is a classic example).

The fifteenth century, as McLuhan saw it—and this was also the century of the birth of the printing press—was the time when what he termed *visual space* was invented and the sense of sight was stepped up and favored out of all proportion to the other sense ratios. This created a visual bias, both in print—with its one-dimensional lines of uniform text, as Vilem Flusser would put it[87]—and in painting with the new mathematics of depth perspective. The audile-tactile sense ratios receded from the Western Clearing until, with the advent and harnessing of electricity—beginning with the telegraph in the 1830s—they were retrieved once more and began to slowly undermine the Gutenbergian Galaxy with what McLuhan called *acoustic space*[88] (a perhaps not so fortunate phrase, since the electric epoch favors the Image over the Word, as Leonard Shlain makes clear; McLuhan's original designation of it as *pictorial space* was better and less confusing, since by *visual space* he really meant *abstractly visual space*).[89] But at any rate, by the phrase *acoustic space*, McLuhan meant for his readers to imagine a sort of cavernous space in which information is not linear at all but rather beamed at the individual from all directions simultaneously. This leads eventually to information overload, to which the cognitive response, as McLuhan put it, is pattern recognition, which is used to organize the information in the form of icons, myths and images[90] (hence my own preference for calling it *pictorial space*).

Space, in Modernist Art beginning with the Impressionists of the 1860s—but most especially with Van Gogh and Gauguin—began once again to flatten out into two dimensions while depth perspective disappeared to become a thing of the past.[91] Cezanne, it seems, was the first to paint on curved non-Euclidean space as his ontological manifold. Einstein, in fact, presupposed non-Euclidean space—especially the geometry of Riemann—or curved space, as the very canvas upon which he painted his entire cosmology. In Modernist Art, meanwhile, the Medieval idea of each thing carving out its own space in a tactile way—since the sense of touch is discontinuous, whereas sight forms a continual visual field—resurfaced and became the configuring aesthetic of movements like Cubism and Surrealism.

The New Flesh
(1:21:19 – 1:26:40)

Max is now shown walking between a pair of old railroad tracks—the sloughed off medium that centralized the city that was then *de*-centralized by the automobile—as he approaches a chain link fence with a sign that reads: "KEEP OUT BY ORDER OF THE HARBOUR COMMISSIONERS." The gate is held loosely together by a chain but he is able to push it open enough to squeeze through and makes his way into a shipyard where a rusted and decaying old schooner that has seen its last days is the only boat tied to the dock. (One has the sense here of the old Industrial world as the North's decaying "rust belt" that was obsolesced by the Pacific Shift to Silicon Valley and its electronics industries). He climbs aboard the boat and pulls open one of its creaky doors to enter a gloomy old metal hold, where chains dangle from the ceiling and debris lies strewn all over the floor. There are empty beer bottles scattered about and the dead frame of a mattress that resembles something out of a Jannis Kounellis metal canvas composition.[92] He finds a round container that is full of the ashes of a dead fire and a dirty old mattress that he pulls back against the metal wall upon which to seat himself. He picks up an empty liquor bottle and tosses it aside, and then sees, with some vestige of hope, a Marlboro package but is dismayed to find it empty and throws it down in disgust.

Max rubs his forehead with his right hand, indicating that the Videodrome-induced headaches are growing worse. But a final hallucination now appears before him in the form of his old television console, now located directly across from him. The image onscreen is of Nicki Brand, wearing her original red dress with long auburn hair.

He tells her that he was hoping she'd be back and she replies that she is now here to guide him, since she has learned a lot since she has last seen him. She claims that she has learned that death is not the end and that she can help him.

He tells her that he doesn't know where he is now and that he is having trouble finding his way about. (For his private identity has been completely scrapped by the new medium of the Videodrome signal).

She explains to him that is because he has gone just about as far as he can with the way things are and that Videodrome still exists and is still very complex. He has hurt them but he has not destroyed them, and to do that he will have to go on to the next phase. He asks her what phase she is talking about, and she explains that his body has already done a lot of changing, but that is only the beginning of the new flesh. Now he needs to take it all the way into a total transformation and asks him if he thinks he's ready, to which he assents.

Then she says that to become the new flesh, he first has to kill the old flesh. But she reassures him not to be afraid to let his physical body die. She tells him to watch and that she will show him what to do. It's easy.

The image on the television screen now shows Max standing inside the same ship in front of a fire blazing in the fire pit, his right hand in the biomechanical form of the new flesh as he puts the gun-hand assemblage to his head and pulls the trigger. At once the television spews forth chunks of organs, blood, entrails and other biological matter.

Max now understands what he has to do. He must replace his physical body with a televisual one, just the way Nicki has done. He will therefore be able to join her in the electronic afterlife configured by Videodrome. (Just as Case, at the end of *Neuromancer*, is able to join the electronic avatar of his dead girlfriend Linda Lee in the Matrix forever).

The next shot shows him standing before a lighted fire, before which he kneels like a penitent, puts the biomechanical gun to his head and says, "Long live the New Flesh," and then pulls the trigger.

The screen fades to black as the sound of his gunshot is heard.

Now the original idea—since it is still found in vestigial form in the novelization—seems to have been that the New Flesh was the actual *physical* alteration and transformation of Max's body so that the hallucinations gradually took on biological reality. The scene in the novelization describing Harlan's death, for instance, shows him horrified to see the actual slit in Max's torso,[93] and the author Jack Martin has Barry Convex at the moment of his murder actually *see* Max's biomechanical gun hand.[94] So I think the original intent, which is consistent with Cronenberg's ontology in films like *The Brood* or *The Fly*, is that the Videodrome signal, taken in massive doses, actually causes the physical soma of the body to change and transform, to grow new organs and appendages like something out of a William Burroughs novel (one of Cronenberg's favorite writers).

But in the film as it stands, this idea was obviously scrapped since Max is shown at the Spectacular Optical trade show *without* his biomechanical hand until the moment of Convex's murder, and he is shown aboard the boat when he first enters it without it as well. So I think the new organs remain hallucinations all the way to the film's conclusion.

Instead, the new flesh becomes the trading out of cells, molecules and atoms—the physical body—for a two-dimensional body made out of electrons and photons. *That* is the new flesh that Nicki Brand is talking about. He will join her in the televisual afterlife of Videodrome (in the novelization, there is another scene never filmed in which Max arrives at the schooner earlier, where he sees the dead avatars of his partners Moses and Raphael, in addition to Masha and Nicki Brand,[95] so the idea is clearly that the only afterlife available to him is the one made out of electrons that constitutes the *inside* of the world of Videodrome, its entire subtle reality).

The ritual transformation that Nicki guides him through in this scene is meant to contrast with the one that Bianca O'Blivion put him through when she actually *did* alter him physically—or at least altered his "imaginal body"—by using the Videodrome signal to confer new weapons upon him: a *vagina dentata* and a gun that shoots not bullets but tiny cancerous tumors.

Nicki Brand as Bianca's counterpole puts him through a *second* ritual transformation—especially made clear by his kneeling in front of the fire like a penitent man—that involves the complete *shedding* of his physical body just the way a cicada leaves behind its empty shell on a tree branch, and in its place he is transformed into the New Flesh of a subtle body that will survive as a two-dimensional avatar—just as the electronic avatars of dead celebrities survive eternally within the electronic arena of all our media apparatuses—inside Videodrome.

Thus: Bianca O'Blivion's transformation of Max was to turn him into the video word made flesh.

Nicki Brand's transformation of Max is to turn him into the New Flesh.

He has now shed his physical body—just as all once living celebrities who are now dead have done—to take up his eternal residence in the electromagnetic sheath of dead celebrities and avatars that now surrounds the earth as a kind of extension of the human nervous system, complete with the ghosts and phantoms that constitute its disembodied voices, images and avatars.

In the end, the Word has become the New Body Electric.

Notes

On Luminous Screens & Other Neuron / Electron Assemblages

1. Vilem Flusser, *Post-History*, trans. Rodrigo Maltez Novaes (Minneapolis, MN: Univocal Publishing, 2013), 91.

2. See John David Ebert, *Post-Classic Cinema* (New York: Create Space, 2013).

3. See Jean Baudrillard, "The Ecstacy of Communication" in Hal Foster, ed. *The Anti-Aesthetic: Essays on Postmodern Culture* (CA: The New Press, 2002), 146.

4. Ibid., 148.

5. See Jean Baudrillard, "The Precession of Simulacra," in *Simulations*, trans. Paul Foss, Paul Patton and Philip Beitchman (Los Angeles: Semiotexte, 1983), 1ff.

6. For my account of this incident and its cultural phenomenology see John David Ebert, *Dead Celebrities, Living Icons: Tragedy and Fame in the Age of the Multimedia Superstar* (New York: Praeger / Greenwood, 2010), 109-112.

7. See the chapter, "Ronald Reagan: the Celluloid Man Made Flesh," ibid., 131ff.

8. Vilem Flusser, ibid., 93.

9. See Walter Benjamin, "The Work of Art in the Age of Mechanical Reproduction" in *Illuminations: Essays and Reflections*, (NY: Harcourt, Brace, Jovanovitch: 1968), 217ff.

10. Jean Baudrillard, *Simulations*, ibid.

11. "This theme enters into the very texture of medieval thought and sensibility, as in the technique of the 'gloss' to release the light from within the text, the technique of illumination as light *through*, not *on*, and the very mode of Gothic architecture itself." Marshall McLuhan, *The Gutenberg Galaxy: The Making of Typographic Man*, (University of Toronto Press, 2011), 121.

12. Marshall McLuhan and Quention Fiore, *The Medium is the Massage: An Inventory of Effects* (NY: Bantam Books, 1965), 20.

13. John David Ebert, *The New Media Invasion: Digital Technologies and the World They Unmake* (Jefferson, NC: McFarland & Co., 2011), 19-21.

14. Joseph Campbell, *The Mythic Image* (Princeton, NJ: Princeton University Press, 1990), 361.

15. Slavoj Zizek, *The Plague of Fantasies* (London & NY: Verso Books, 2009).

16. Cornelius Castoriadis, *The Imaginary Institution of Society* (UK: Polity Press, 2005), 135ff.

17. Cornelius Castoriadis, *Philosophy, Politics, Autonomy* (London & NY: Oxford University Press, 1991), 13ff.

18. For a wonderful take on consumer society as seen through the lens of the myth of Plato's Cave, see Jose Saramago, *The Cave*, trans. Margaret Costa (Orlando, FL: Mariner Books, 2002).

19. Andrew Niccol's screenplay for *The Truman Show* was clearly inspired by Philip K. Dick's 1958 novel *Time Out of Joint*.

20. Jean Baudrillard, *Telemorphosis*, trans. Drew S. Burk (Minneapolis, MN: Univocal Publishing, 2011).

Opening Title Sequence

21. See essay #15, "Notes on the Media as Art Forms," in Marshall McLuhan, *McLuhan Unbound* (Corte Madeira, CA: Gingko Press, 2005), 9. But see also essay #18 in the same series, "Myth and Mass Media," where on page 14 he states: "...in television the striking fact is that the image is defined by light *through*, not by light *on*. It is this fact that separates television from photography and movie, relating it profoundly to stained glass."

22. For the concept of assemblages, see the chapter "Introduction: Rhizome" in Gilles Deleuze and Felix Guattari, *A Thousand Plateaus: Capitalism and Schizophrenia*, trans. Brian Massumi (University of Minnesota Press, 1987), 3ff.

23. Gunther Anders, "The World as Phantom and as Matrix: Philosophical Considerations on Radio and Television" to be found online at: https://libcom.org/book/export/html/51647

24. Neil Postman, *The Disappearance of Childhood* (NY: Vintage Books, 1994). McLuhan, however, was there first, for he remarked that "the child was an invention of the seventeenth century." See Marshall McLuhan and Quentin Fiore, *The Medium is the Massage: An Inventory of Effects*, ibid., 8.

Samurai Dreams

25. Marshall McLuhan, *Understanding Media: The Extensions of Man* (Cambridge, MA: MIT Press, 1994), 8.

26. See "You Tube and the Twilight of Copyright," in John David Ebert, *The New Media Invasion*, ibid., 40ff.

27. Peter Sloterdijk, "Rules for the Human Zoo: a Response to the Letter on Humanism," *Environment and*

Planning D: Society and Space, 2009, vol. 27, 12-18. For the concept of "disinhibiting media" see esp. 15-16.

Harlan

28. The real address of the building where Civic TV was supposed to be located was 6 Wellington Street, Toronto, Ontario, Canada.

29. See the chapter entitled "Howard Hughes, the World's First Serial Crash Artist," in John David Ebert, *Dead Celebrities, Living Icons*, ibid., 13.

30. As Heidegger remarks, "Television epitomizes all removal of distance, and will soon pervade and dominate the gears and bustle of all interaction." See "Bremen Lectures: *Insight into That Which Is*" (1949) in Gunter Figal, ed. *The Heidegger Reader*, trans. Jerome Veith, (Bloomington & Indianapolis: Indiana University Press, 2009), esp. 253-54.

31. "Any highway eatery with its tv set, newspaper, and magazine is as cosmopolitan as New York or Paris," is how he puts it in Marshall McLuhan, *Counterblast 1954 Edition* (Berkeley & Hamburg: Gingko Press, 2011), no page numbers.

32. See "WikiLeaks and the Death of Culture" in John David Ebert, *The New Media Invasion,* ibid., esp. 89.

33. See "Art at War" in Boris Groys, *Art Power*, (Cambridge, MA: MIT Press, 2008), esp. 122.

34. See "A Final Word" in John David Ebert, *Art After Metaphysics*, (New York: Create Space, 2013), 215-18.

The Rena King Show

35. See the essay "One Thousand Malkoviches: Reflections on the Cultural Phenomenology of Celebrity"

in John David Ebert, *Cultural Decay Rate: Essays on Contemporary Art, Literature and Social Disintegration* (New York: Create Space, 2015), 139ff.

36. Boris Groys, *Art Power*, ibid., 125.

Pittsburgh

37. Marshall McLuhan, letter to Clare Westcott, November 26, 1975. *Letters of Marshall McLuhan*, Matie Molinaro, Corinne McLuhan, William Toye, eds. (Oxford University Press, 1987), 514.

Nicki Brand

38. Gilles Deleuze, *Difference and Repetition*, trans. Paul Patton (New York: Columbia University Press, 1994), 244-47.

39. The concept of the Body without Organs is elaborated in the chapter entitled "November 28, 1947: How Do You Make Yourself a Body without Organs?" in Deleuze & Guattari, *A Thousand Plateaus*, ibid., 149ff.

Masha

40. Jean Baudrillard, *Telemorphosis*, ibid., 48.

41. Thus echoing the title of McLuhan's essay, "At the moment of Sputnik the planet became a global theater in which there are no spectators but only actors," *Journal of Communication*, vol. 4, issue 1, March, 1974, 48-58.

Cigarette Burn

42. Marshall McLuhan and Quentin Fiore, *The Medium is the Massage*, ibid., 125.

43. See the chapter "Andy Warhol's Cult of the Dead Celebrity," in John David Ebert, *Dead Celebrities, Living Icons*, ibid., 83ff.

Max and Masha

44. Harold Innis's media studies breakthrough was *Empire and Communications*, based on six lectures that he delivered at Oxford University in 1948. This was the seminal book that inspired McLuhan to shift the direction of his studies from the content of a medium—which he focused on in his first book *The Mechanical Bride* (1951)—to the bias of the medium itself and how it distorts the message that goes through it. For the most recent edition, see Harold Innis, *Empire and Communications*, (Toronto, Ontario, Canada: Dundern Press, Ltd., 2007) and also *The Bias of Communication* (University of Toronto Press, 1951).

45. I originated the concept of the metaphysical vulva, which may be found articulated in the "Introduction to the Metaphysical Vulva" in John David Ebert, *Alien Scene-by-Scene* (New York: Create Space, 2015), 11-21.

46. McLuhan's dig at the Shannon-Weaver model (1948) is indirect, but it may be found in essay #15, "Notes on the Media as Art Forms," page 6, dating from 1954 and collected in *McLuhan Unbound*, ibid.

Cathode Ray Mission

47. The address where Cronenberg filmed his Cathode Ray Mission is 125 Bathurst Street, Toronto, Ontario, Canada.

48. See especially Marshall McLuhan and Harley Parker,

Through the Vanishing Point: Space in Poetry and Painting (New York: Harper Colophon Books, 1969).

49. See Marshall McLuhan, *Understanding Me: Lectures and Interviews*, Stephanie McLuhan and David Staines, eds. (Cambridge, MA: MIT Press, 2003), 101.

The Videocassette

50. Jack Martin, *Videodrome: a Novel Based on a Screenplay by David Cronenberg* (New York: Zebra Books, 1983), 114.
51. Ibid., 104-07.
52. Marshall McLuhan, *Understanding Me*, ibid., 94.

Archives

53. "…at this moment, we are on the air, and on the air we do not have any physical body. When you're on the telephone or on radio or on TV, you don't have a physical body. You're just an image on the air. When you don't have a physical body, you are a discarnate being." Marshall McLuhan, *Understanding Me: Lectures and Interviews*, ibid., 268.
54. Jean Baudrillard, *The Intelligence of Evil, or the Lucidity Pact* (London, UK: Bloomsbury, 2013), 151.
55. Jean Baudrillard, "The Ecstacy of Communication" in Hal Foster, ed. *The Anti-Aesthetic: Essays on Postmodern Culture*, ibid., 149.

Gun / Orifice

56. John David Ebert, *Cultural Decay Rate*, ibid., 110-11.

57. Martin Heidegger, *Introduction to Metaphysics*, trans. Gregory Fried and Richard Polt, (New Haven and London: Yale University Press, 2000), 143.

58. Peter Sloterdijk, "Rules for the Human Zoo," ibid. 15-16.

Barry Convex

59. The real life address of the exterior of Max Renn's apartment is the Fleetwood Apartments, 64 St. Clair Ave., W., Toronto, Ontario, Canada.

60. Jack Martin, *Videodrome*, ibid. 177.

61. Though this scene was actually filmed, it didn't make the final cut, but can be found on YouTube at: https://www.youtube.com/watch?v=IyvGqhw8HtE

62. Jack Martin, *Videodrome*, ibid., 175-76.

63. Ibid., 179-80.

64. Ibid., 180.

65. Ibid., 181.

66. William Irwin Thompson, *The American Replacement of Nature: Everyday Acts and Outrageous Evolution of Economic Life* (New York: Doubleday, 1991).

67. Morris Berman, *A Question of Values* (New York: Create Space, 2010).

68. Cornelius Castoriadis, *The Imaginary Institution of Society*, ibid. 135ff.

69. See "258. The veneration of icons and iconoclasm" in Mircea Eliade, *A History of Religious Ideas, volume 3: From Muhammad to the Age of Reforms* (University of Chicago Press, 1985), 59-61.

70. I originated the concept of the "Boundary Act" in Chapter Eight, "The AUM Shinrikyo Nerve Gas Attacks and their Attempt to Recode Japanese Society," in John

David Ebert, *The Age of Catastrophe: Disaster and Humanity in Modern Times* (Jefferson, NC and London: 2012), 104.

Corpse / Corpuscles

71. Jack Martin, *Videodrome*, ibid., 203.
72. Vilem Flusser, *Into Immaterial Culture*, trans. Rodrigo Malez Novaes (UK: Metaflux Publishing, 2015).

Programming Max

73. For my earlier reading of *Videodrome* see John David Ebert, *Celluloid Heroes & Mechanical Dragons: Film as the Mythology of Electronic Society* (Christchurch, New Zealand: Cybereditions, 2005), 73-74.

Gun Embryo

74. Marshall McLuhan and Quentin Fiore, *The Medium is the Massage*, ibid., 25-41.
75. Marshall McLuhan, *Understanding Media*, ibid., 64.
76. See the entry under "Dromosphere" in John Armitage, ed. *The Virilio Dictionary* (Edinburgh University Press, 2013), 75-76.

Spree Killer

77. Jack Martin, *Videodrome*, ibid., 219.
78. The interested reader can find my accounts of all these incidents in John David Ebert, *Dead Celebrities, Living Icons*, ibid.
79. See the essay "The Historical Development of Mythology" in Joseph Campbell, *The Mythic Dimension:*

Selected Essays 1959-1987, Antony Van Couvering, ed. (New York: Harper Collins, 1997), esp. 20-22.

80. See my review of the film in John David Ebert, *Post-Classic Cinema: Collected Film Reviews 2005-2013* (New York: Create Space, 2013), 195ff.

The Video Word Made Flesh

81. See Hans Belting, *Likeness and Presence: A History of the Image Before the Era of Art*, trans. Edmund Jephcott (University of Chicago Press, 1994), 33-34.

Killing Harlan

82. Robert Graves, *The White Goddess: A Historical Grammar of Poetic Myth* (New York: Farrar, Straus and Giroux, 2013), 365.

Spring Trade Show

83. Joseph Campbell and Bill Moyers, *The Power of Myth*, Betty Sue Flowers, ed. (New York: Anchor Books, 1991), 233.

84. See "Intermezzo: The Birth of the Movie Theater Out of Arabian Optics" in John David Ebert, *Celluloid Heroes & Mechanical Dragons*, ibid., 213-14.

85. See essay #2, "The Effect of the Printed Book on Language in the 16th Century," in *McLuhan Unbound*, ibid.

86. See especially the introductory essay "Sensory Modes" in Marshall McLuhan and Harley Parker, *Through the Vanishing Point*, ibid., esp. 8-16.

87. See the essay "The Codified Word" in Vilem Flusser, *Writings*, Andreas Strohl, ed., trans. Erik Eisel (University of

Minnesota Press, 2002), 35ff.

88. For acoustic space, see Marshall McLuhan, *The Gutenberg Galaxy*, ibid., 368.

89. So far as I know, the earliest occurrence of the use of the phrase "acoustic space" in McLuhan's writings, as opposed to what he had been calling "pictorial space" in his earlier work, dates from the 1956 essay "The Media Fit the Battle of Jericho," which is essay #16 in *McLuhan Unbound*, ibid., where he writes on page 7: "The oral and acoustic space of tribal cultures had never met a visual reconstruction of the past." Whereas in the 1954 essay, "The New Media as Political Forms," he is still referring to the "non-literate" cultures of China and India as "almost entirely oral and pictographic." This quote is from page 12 of essay #4 in *McLuhan Unbound*, ibid.

90. "You cannot cope with vast amounts of information in the old fragmentary classified patterns. You tend to go looking for mythic and structural forms in order to manage such complex data moving at very high speeds." See Marshall McLuhan, *Understanding Me: Lectures and Interviews,* ibid., 63.

91. See "On the Four World Ages of European Art" in John David Ebert, *Art After Metaphysics*, ibid.

The New Flesh

92. See Jannis Kounellis, "Untitled 1984/87," which is a metal canvas that features a similar empty bed frame.

93. Jack Martin, *Videodrome*, ibid., 243.

94. Ibid., 249.

95. Ibid., 227-30.

Bibliography

Anders, Gunther. "The World as Phantom and as Matrix: Philosophical Considerations on Radio and Television." : https://libcom.org/book/export/html/51647

Armitage, John, ed. *The Virilio Dictionary*. Edinburgh University Press, 2013.

Baudrillard, Jean. *The Intelligence of Evil, or the Lucidity Pact*. London, UK: Bloomsbury, 2013.

____. *Simulations*. Los Angeles: Semiotexte, 1983.

____. *Telemorphosis*. Trans. Drew S. Burk. Minneapolis, MN: Univocal Publishing, 2011.

Belting, Hans. *Likeness and Presence: A History of the Image Before the Era of Art*. Trans. Edmund Jephcott. University of Chicago Press, 1994.

Benjamin, Walter. *Illuminations: Essays and Reflections*. NY: Harcourt, Brace, Jovanovitch, 1968.

Berman, Morris. *A Question of Values*. NY: Create Space, 2010.

Campbell, Joseph. *The Mythic Dimension: Selected Essays 1959-1987*. Antony van Couvering, ed. NY: Harper Collins, 1997.

____. *The Mythic Image*. Princeton, NJ: Princeton University Press, 1990.

____, and Moyers, Bill. *The Power of Myth*. Betty Sue Flowers, ed. NY: Anchor Books, 1991.

Castoriadis, Cornelius. *The Imaginary Institution of*

Society. UK: Polity Press, 2005.

___. *Philosophy, Politics, Autonomy*. London & NY: Oxford University Press, 1991.

Deleuze, Gilles. *Difference and Repetition*. Trans. Paul Patton. NY: Columbia University Press, 1994.

___, and Guattari, Felix. *A Thousand Plateaus: Capitalism and Schizophrenia*. Trans. Brian Massumi. University of Minnesota Press, 1987.

Ebert, John David. *The Age of Catastrophe: Disaster and Humanity in Modern Times*. Jefferson, NC and London: 2012.

___. *Alien Scene-by-Scene*. NY: Create Space, 2015.

___. *Art After Metaphysics*. NY: Create Space, 2013.

___. *Celluloid Heroes & Mechanical Dragons: Film as the Mythology of Electronic Society*. Christchurch, New Zealand: Cybereditions, 2005.

___. *Cultural Decay Rate: Essays on Contemporary Art, Literature and Social Disintegration*. NY: Create Space, 2015.

___. *Dead Celebrities, Living Icons: Tragedy and Fame in the Age of the Multimedia Superstar*. NY: Praeger / Greenwood, 2010.

___. *The New Media Invasion: Digital Technologies and the World They Unmake*. Jefferson, NC: McFarland & Co., 2011.

___. *Post-Classic Cinema*. NY: Create Space, 2013.

Eliade, Mircea. *The History of Religious Ideas, Volume 3: From Muhammad to the Age of Reforms*. University of Chicago Press, 1985.

Figal, Gunter, ed. *The Heidegger Reader*. Trans. Jerome Veith. Bloomington & Indianapolis: Indiana University Press, 2009.

Flusser, Vilem. *Into Immaterial Culture*. Trans. Rodrigo Maltez Novaes. UK: Metaflux Publishing, 2015.

___. *Post-History*. Trans. Rodrigo Maltez Novaes. Minneapolis, MN: Univocal Publishing, 2013.

___. *Writings*. Andreas Strohl, ed. Trans. Erik Eisel. University of Minnesota Press, 2002.

Graves, Robert. *The White Goddes: A Historical Grammar of Poetic Myth*. NY: Farrar, Straus and Giroux, 2013.

Foster, Hal, ed. *The Anti-Aesthetic: Essays on Postmodern Culture*. CA: The New Press, 2002.

Groys, Boris. *Art Power*. Cambridge, MA: MIT Press, 2008.

Heidegger, Martin. *Introduction to Metaphysics*. Trans. Gregory Fried and Richard Polt. New Haven and London: Yale University Press, 2000.

Innis, Harold. *The Bias of Communication*. University of Toronto Press, 1951.

___. *Empire and Communications*. Toronto, Ontario, Canada: Dundern Press, Ltd., 2007.

Martin, Jack. *Videodrome: a Novel Based on a Screenplay by David Cronenberg*. NY: Zebra Books, 1983.

McLuhan, Marshall. "At the moment of Sputnik the planet became a global theater in which there are no spectators but only actors." *Journal of Communication*, vol. 4, issue 1, March, 1974.

___. *Counterblast 1954 Edition*. Berkeley & Hamburg: Gingko Press, 2011.

___. *The Gutenberg Galaxy: The Making of Typographic Man*. University of Toronto Press, 2011.

___. *Letters of Marshall McLuhan*, Matie Molinaro, Corinne McLuhan, William Toye, eds. Oxford University Press, 1987.

___. *McLuhan Unbound*. Corte Madeira, CA: Gingko Press, 2005.

___. *The Mechanical Bride: Folklore of Industrial Man*.

Boston, MA: Beacon Press, 1967.

___. *Understanding Me: Lectures and Interviews*. Stephanie McLuhan and David Staines, eds. Cambridge, MA: MIT Press, 2005.

___. *Understanding Media: The Extensions of Man*. Cambridge, MA: MIT Press, 1994.

___, and Harley Parker. *Through the Vanishing Point: Space in Poetry and Painting*. NY: Harper Colophon Books, 1969.

___, and Quentin Fiore. *The Medium is the Massage: An Inventory of Effects*. NY: Bantam Books, 1965.

Postman, Neil. *The Disappearance of Childhood*. NY: Vintage Books, 1994.

Saramago, Jose. *The Cave*. Trans. Margaret Costa. Orlando, FL: Mariner Books, 2002.

Shlain, Leonard. *The Alphabet vs. The Goddess: The Conflict Between Word and Image*. NY: Penguin Books, 1999.

Sloterdijk, Peter. "Rules for the Human Zoo: a Response to the Letter on Humanism." *Environment and Planning D: Society and Space*, vol. 27, 2009.

Thompson, William Irwin. *The American Replacement of Nature: Everyday Acts and Outrageous Evolution of Economic Life*. NY: Doubleday, 1991.

Zizek, Slavoj. *The Plague of Fantasies*. London & NY: Verso Books, 2009.

Printed in Great Britain
by Amazon